Visiting the Eastern Uplands

Visiting the Eastern Uplands

Maine Metaphor

S. Dorman

RESOURCE *Publications* · Eugene, Oregon

VISITING THE EASTERN UPLANDS
Maine Metaphor

Copyright © 2016 S. Dorman. All rights reserved. Except for brief quotations in critical publications or reviews, no part of this book may be reproduced in any manner without prior written permission from the publisher. Write: Permissions, Wipf and Stock Publishers, 199 W. 8th Ave., Suite 3, Eugene, OR 97401.

Resource Publications
An Imprint of Wipf and Stock Publishers
199 W. 8th Ave., Suite 3
Eugene, OR 97401

www.wipfandstock.com

PAPERBACK ISBN: 978-1-5326-0311-2
HARDCOVER ISBN: 978-1-5326-0313-6
EBOOK ISBN: 978-1-5326-0312-9

Manufactured in the U.S.A.   NOVEMBER 2, 2016

For Gideon, who helps things grow

Contents

Preface | ix

Old-Time Celebrations | 1

Flight to the Eastern Uplands | 7

Life in the Highlands, Where Pipers Call | 17

Departure | 26

Future Maine | 30

CQ from Maine | 35

Hurricane Tree | 38

Father Word | 41

Going North beneath the Moon | 44

Breakfast at the ELM TREE | 47

Aroostook County, Ohio | 50

Monuments | 54

Touring Presque Isle | 58

The Aroostook Room | 62

Broccoli Bombers | 66

The Borderland | 72

Industry on the Borderline | 79

The Excesses and Economies of Travel | 82

Where Eagles Feed | 90

Logger Activists | 95

Contents

Good Work | 98

The Caribou Loams | 103

"So It's Not Home" | 107

Mars Hill | 110

Prose and Dreams | 114

Uplands Interlude | 117
    Alone in the Western Mountains
    Second "Flight" to the Eastern Uplands
    A Wheel within the Wheel of Making
    What Am I Doing in Aroostook?
    Slow-Boating Aroostook in Air
    Girl Power
    Home, Waiting

Ohio, Maine. Again | 136
    August 1, 2015
    August 2, 2015 Sunday a.m.

Monday, August 3, 2015 Mountain Glory Farm, 4:15 a.m. | 143

On the Military Road to Houlton? | 148

Moving Southwest beneath the Sun | 153
    August 5, 2015, home in the western mountains

Preface

GROWN IN THE WRITING, this book in your hands has thrown out unexpected roots and branches into our long lives. This is the third book in the cycle of *Maine Metaphor* but it began in the second book as a yearning to see Aroostook County, The County as it's called here in Maine. So that the first part of this particular book was initially part of *Experience in the Western Mountains*. This book is a pruning or scion, cut from the other. But there was not enough of it.

Now the present book opens in our Town in the mountains, as close as convenient in narrative time to our initial Aroostook discoveries. I tried to keep its theme—food, eating, and nourishment—pen in hand, from the beginning. With its uplands material being too slender to sustain a published volume, more was needed.

Two additional trips were made, one alone, camping, reading secondhand finds, and scribbling in a private journal. That journal was not at first meant for publication but has since been adapted, personalizing the formal Aroostook narrative. Afterward, together, Allen and I made another uplands venture. These journeys occurred 17 and 25 years after our initial necessarily brief exploration. I wrote them out to complete the book but that is not why I made these trips. I simply wanted to experience the Eastern Uplands again. And there was the recent migration of Amish to my "Ohio-land" in Maine. I wanted to see them in the Maine upland. I wanted it all, and subsequently "all" was also written out.

As always, our experience was the real interest. Writing it and working out the metaphor with research and meditation was the laborious part, not so rewarding to me as the experience itself. If there are any—readers may find that aging has removed some of my former boldness, and some crafted overbold tonal qualities. For, as my younger self writes—while ignorant of our experience ahead—only later do we realize that the watchers judging

Preface

us will be ourselves. "We are the judges who can't help but gauge the performance in our execution of life's turns." It will look different when we've been made watchful by our experience.

Old-Time Celebrations

We stood in burning sun, this gathering awaiting the parade. A sheriff's car crested the hill above and began slow descent toward us, followed closely by walkers with flags. Now they stopped, poised, unmoving; and so we stood back, unmoving ourselves. Then came the unexpected, evocative: the remote skirling of pipes beyond the crest, out of sight—drawing us powerfully. In twos and threes we ventured onto the skirt of the roadway, straining toward the haunting sound. Faint at first, it was nonetheless an unmistakable call. Nothing save a bag with chanter and three pipes (flared and sounding with the breath of the piper) could make that distinctive wail and drone—though the pipers could not be seen.

We stand rooted to the sand shoulder, watching for them as they approach, still out of sight. Increasing in vibration, volume. The unseen sounding has a mesmeric quality derived from pulsing constancy of the base drone. This is overlaid by varying notes of other pipes. Measured staccato of the accompanying drums anchors the rhythm in our rapt souls. Now we see them—in colorful kilts, sporrans and glengarrys—coming toward us: a little band playing with nimble fingers, tendons flexing in their forearms as they sway by.

Passing through the town-gathering, pipers came alongside us, excluding all distraction with this call. Passing . . . and our heads turning, our necks craning; they rounded the corner behind town hall, passing away. . . . Out of sound and sight. We knew then that the parade was gone. That anything to come, though charming, would be but anti-climactic.

Yet many fair floats came after because, this being the 175th anniversary celebration of our green town, the themes were necessarily historical. They pointed community life as it had been founded and lived. First came two settlers in horse-drawn cart, represented in the actual descendents of

Visiting the Eastern Uplands

William and Martha Yates, a Scotsman and his wife who, first, hacked out a presumably God-fearing home on a rocky height in the green center of town. It's a place now owned by a Paper Concern—overgrown and deserted except for deer, bear, moose and other wild creatures making their homes among mountainous slopes, honeycombed with settlers' crumbling stone foundational walls. Highland pipers, calling from a height, seem a true choice to lead this particular parade downhill—solemnly toward us.

It was the fullest, richest parade I'd seen since coming to Maine. Floating exhibits included tableaux of logging, lumbering, milling, wood-turning, farming, domestic arts, resorts, sports and recreation; the one-room school lumbering along on a flatbed float, children in period-costume, seated at their old-time desks before the teacher, Colista Morgan,. (Mrs. Morgan, local writer, actually taught in the one-room school nearby.) All are typical Maine scenes, many dating to 175 years ago, whose descent is with us today, still largely comprising the content of our area's economy. These heritage displays show forth our town's creative gratitude.

Last of the parade came Desert Storm, our recent battles in the Middle East. A shining fire truck with names of our town's three Storm veterans emblazoned on a computer-generated banner and taped to the side of the tanker. Two young men in camouflage fatigues and riding high in the cab were vets—all unknown to me. As they passed so near, I felt a slight embarrassment even though voluntary military service is also traditional here. Young Mainers, forced by lack of opportunity and jobs have for several generations opted for Government Issue. Now these two passed this spectator in a vacuum of silence for I did not know how to honor their participation in the Storm. The climate of the national culture demanded cheers. For our financial interests we'd gone to aid allies held captive. Yet, silent bewildered solemnity seemed the appropriate response. Had I known the three Gulf veterans personally, I would have cheered. Personal emotion would transform the symbolic nature of an otherwise uneasy encounter.

It's late and silent, up here where I walk above the little village of our rural town. The parade, with its historical legacy, passed by many hours ago in bright morning. The neighbors have all gone, the few houses of my little neighborhood empty and dark below. Everyone's gone to the fireworks display one town over, and Boots—the old dog—and I are winding up Deer Hill Road. Upon the flat up there in the dark I, too, might see the fireworks.

Old-Time Celebrations

Five miles away over the old hills lies the village of our nearest neighbor, Canada, Maine. Its townline abuts ours and we will soon cross that line as we climb. I wonder if the hills will permit a view of the display, which is planned as an apology for last week's foul-up. Almost every community in Maine knows some form of summertime festival. Last week Canada was to have one of its parades—topped off with a fireworks salute. But it was canceled (after the crowd assembled) when the fireworks company failed to show. "We take full responsibility for the mix-up which was completely our fault. So *We Will Make It up to You!* ran the three-quarter page ad in the local weekly. "We will surpass every past celebration to say we are really sorry."

As we near the flat where the view opens out, from a distance comes the first emphatic *boom!!* The opening signal. I quicken my step, tighten up a bit on his leash, urge the dog on. As we emerge from behind the large u-shaped house, built to take advantage of this view, we see the first spouts of colored fire shooting up from the dark hills; hear its thunder, far away, born with force through the airways of the Western Mountains. I stand in the road—looking out across the valley toward richly blazoning sparks. There are the distant landmarks, particularly the lights of ridge-side condos, in Canada, Maine.

The artistic u-shaped house is dark and I don't know whether the owner and his family are out-of-state or at the celebration. Possessed of this fine large second home, they are rarely here. The father is a Scotsman, complete with rich Gaelic accent. (But can he play bagpipes?) I checked the landscape for thistles honoring his heritage and find none. The significance of the Scottish symbol eludes me at the moment—something to do with gratitude for comfort or aid. His home sits precisely where the dog and I used to stand to take this view. These days I stand in the road or perch on a rock across the way.

I seek one now and, tugging on the leash, make my way over to it. This jumble of freshly dug rock glimmers, lambent in clear bright dusk of a summer's eve. The rocks haven't yet become engulfed by lichens—which darken in slowly plundering the rock.

I settle on the brightest rock because it gives unobstructed view to this drama of fireworks blazing across the valley. In our lengthy summer dusk, trees opposite the road are dark and lacy-looking against the lighter sky. A breeze rustles black leaves, but not enough to sway slender stems. The seven or eight successive layers of hills between here and tallest *Agiocachook* have blended into one dim ridge, and the fireworks—fountains of green and red, orange and golden white—spout up from below against that dark mass. A faint purple hush of haze lingers upon the contour of mountains. In the northwest, blue faint light of a lost sun persists, silhouetting the hills that are next neighbor to our own block of hills.

I sit quietly, watching pinwheels and fountains; spheres with red tops and green bottoms; Jupiters of color and light—fiery glints thrown up by artists. Some so bright they flash lightning on rocks beside me.

Sound often comes when color is gone, owing to the difference in visual and aural waves. Distant *booms* and *boks* kindle imaginings of giants slamming their doors. A husband and wife, striding the mountaintops, in fits and fights. It's a contest, a battle not so much between sexes as between egos.

Boots hears them and is afraid. He's hard of hearing now and so hears only when it's extra loud. Then he stands, restive, and starts to wander off. I call him back, recollecting his fear of thunder, of fireworks, and of how that fear came into him.

It was a Fourth of July gathering, when a very strange drunk threw a firecracker into the dark—*ka-boom!!* Careless in drink, he threw it at the dark dog tied up among shadows, away from the gathering. The dog yelped and cried. And so did the drunken stranger. He cried and cried and wished to God he'd never done it. Over the years since then the dog has gone temporarily insane over thunder, fireworks, fire arms, rumbling pulp trucks, anything. Shiver and howl, tear up the ground, rip the door apart. Now he is hard of hearing and half blind. Sometimes it's hard to get his attention because of this physical deterioration. I call and call, but he continues in the wrong direction. Yet I have discovered something good out of all his distress. The dog hears, he obeys me, when I clap my hands—*bang!*

As promised, the show is a long one. But I'm not a kid anymore. I've seen my share of such displays and find my attention wandering. I'm just too impatient for the grand finale, a favorite of this spectacle.

A lightning bug goes blinking by—long cold green flashes, like those used in American Morse code. And, actually, the firefly's display *is* coded and singular, meant to attract a particular species. There are seven codes, one for each species. The male, in the air, is signaling his prospective mate down on the ground. Only she, whose answering precisely matches his, will be selected for his amorous attention. Her cool yellow-green assent, flashing up from the weeds, holds the only attraction. The six other species could flash all night and it would not mean a thing to him.

As I turn my gaze back to the fireworks display, I find myself imagining spectacular battle in the valley five miles away. A thrilling prospect—to witness high desperation, the anguish of armies in flashing brightness, in color and thunder and rain. War, we learned in watching Desert Storm (televised spectacle), is indeed glorious and stimulating to safe spectators. And these fireworks remind me of patriotism. I think of another battle, fought during the War of 1812, which inspired the national anthem that so stirs us on occasion. It's a curious convoluted song in both melody and word, full of powerful imagery: a star-scattered cloth, glaring rockets, glimmering dawn. And once the tune for a bawdy clubbing song in 18th century England. Are its inheritors reverent and grateful yet?

Sitting up here on hard stone, awaiting the grand finale, I want now only to see it and be on my way. It's late, I'm tired, and home beckons me from the valley. I guess I've seen too many such displays....

Then, *popping!!*—it happens. Fire in the mountains, roaring. As though dark distant thickets of pines ignite on tinder lands. Here is the transfixing crescendo, a colored inferno, glancing up in furious might. I watch until it stops in sudden silence, leaving only tiny lights of distant condos where once the fire stood.

I slide off the rock, hook Boots to his leash and start down. But I glance back, startled, into the east—directly opposite the silent spot on the dark blended mountains. Through trees eastward a great brightness dawns, shedding shine across the heavens, dimming lights of stars. My breath is caught and held. It must be the moon, hidden from sight among the woods.

The dog and I descend Deer Hill, and moon's face unseen sends light through the black leafy stems on my left, eastward. Approaching a wall of trees in the curve ahead, I see, not the moon, but its beam upon the trees. And another shaft strikes leaves in the woods—gleaming green light—as I pass: a single long dash like that of a firefly.

Then, as we near home, comes a clearing in the path of its searchbeams. At last I look up to see the moon-face itself. The great round disk has washed its face clean in the light of the sun. All its garments are white.

We keep walking, down toward the house where I will chain up our dog. But my thoughts turn back now to the pipers who played in the morning, who wailed on the pipes. I think back to the drummers who kept time.

Among them was an oddly dressed drum major, beating on the bass drum: boom... *boom*... BOOM!

It was later in the day when they played for the crowd at the foot of Deer Hill Road where the town celebrated its birth. There I got a good look at the drum major's costume. To my untrained eye it was a costume, but later I learned that it was regimental attire for the 48th Canadian Regiment. The drummer's sporran, kilt, and blouse were over-mantled by the skin and head of a leopard, bestowed for valor in combat by an Ethiopian leader. They were playing a song so powerful it made me feel like leaping.

On a night like this, after a day filled with symbols of such mighty heritage, some story-tellers might be drawn to invoke the tale of the Pied Piper. As a kid I worried so about that story. The parents, of children who were lured off, should not have denied the piper his due. To be free of rats deserves a grateful response—but whatever became of those little ones?

Yet now that I'm grown I don't worry about them. Ingrates like those parents might not have raised them so well. The children did better to follow the piper.

Flight to the Eastern Uplands

THE DAY OF THE Eastern Uplands has finally arrived—at least in part. Geographers and geologists may decry my loose use of the term. I adapted it on coming across a version of "Eastern Uplands" while looking at the geological map in Mantor Library at the University of Maine at Farmington: "The Dissected Uplands." Today we plan to explore its southern edge.

I expect that from the air Maine's blueberry barrens will look a flatland, dissected into geometric quilt-works by the impulse for orderliness on the part of agribusiness field owners. But nature has played her part, with glaciers, by scrubbing those uplands of soil and leaving in their wake nothing but plains, bogs, and a few monadnocks. She gave fire to natives, ensuring that lowbush blueberry scrub would always flourish there.

Today is our day to make at least a start on visiting the Eastern Uplands, so long a goal of my hungry creativity. It's also the day of our first *long* flight together after an interval of almost two years. That he keep licensed, keep in practice, Allen and I are flying. We'll fly to an airstrip at Deblois, on the great blueberry barrens in Washington County, at the opposite and eastern end of the state from these Western Mountains. The winds of finance have moderated to allow a writer's junket and chance to brush up on flying skills. Thus, we are now lifting off the runway of Oxford County Airport, and I am feeling the smoothness of takeoff in the rental, a light little Cessna 150. Silently rejoicing.

The green ground drops away. I'm grateful it's easy to ascend and so joyous an act. Yesterday's brief foray in sky was all turbulence and banking and sickening slam-bams. I don't even want to recall it. Timing is all in avoiding turbulence, and yesterday ours was way off. In the a.m. Allen did his three takeoffs and landings (required) and then I hopped in. We flew over Thompson Lake and then turned to intersect the Augusta VOR, a navigational aid. This, while winds of convection played lift-and-slam with the plane. It was only moderate turbulence—so he said. Thus I learned that moderate turbulence is enough to crack me to the core and wither my wits away.

Only a brief flight—up and around and back in no time—but completely deranging while it endured. Depending on currents, the human psyche can be sound one moment and shattered to bits the next. All that was left to me was gratitude that the turbulence had not been "severe" or "extreme."

Consider my paraphrased definition of *Plane and Pilot* magazine's diagram of disturbance rated light through extreme. "Light" may have roll disturbance less than 5°, where control corrections are instantaneous. "Moderate" throws the craft banking up to 30°, moving things about in the cockpit—maybe a passenger's stomach?—and control time will lag. With "severe" you get unresponsive controls with attempted corrections, angles of 50°—you're on your side—and airspeed can shear 25 knots. "Extreme" is rare but you've already lost control when you're rolling past vertical.

Allen has said that under certain conditions it's best not to fight it. Best to let go the controls and allow the plane to right itself.

But I need not think of yesterday's turbulence, for here we are, rising smoothly, quickly, the white farmhouses sinking and diminishing beneath the technical marvel of this craft. We lift above Streakéd Mountain, are banking over firred and rocky ledge . . . now away into the east, into ascending sun. Long shadows stretch across the rich green lawn of Oxford and Androscoggin counties. Looking back, I see our remote tiny shadow trailing over the ground. Lush and golden is this new day, and convection turbulence in early morning atmosphere is nonexistent. If we are fortunate we'll arrive smoothly at the barrens one hundred and ten miles away and depart again before the earth's warming truly begins. With that warming would come devilish convection currents.

Allen touches back on the throttle. The plane slows its ascent. I look down to see green patterns in fields, occasional delicate bogs dotted with trees, dark winding ribbons of streams; and lakes lakes lakes. The ocean, to my right, is but a dim blue guess upon the southern horizon. We cross the dark Andy River, the Belgrade Lakes, this lakey land. A reflection of sun shoots a blinding beam up from shimmering waters, as far as I can see. There's a pool of pure light across the midriff of Cobbosseecontee.

Flight to the Eastern Uplands

Augusta traffic this is 23 Juliet approximately 5 mi. west of the Airport at 2200 ft.

There's the airport, artificially elevated at one end above the white tenuous highway. I look over my shoulder at the green oxidized dome of the Capitol, at that dark band, the Kennebec River, below our wheel. There's the toy traffic moving on avenues of commerce and policy. That's where decisions are made concerning the fate of our water and air, the body of earth. There stewardship over creation in Maine is executed. Back out over the countryside now—the artwork of the pit laborer with his tiny machine. Sculpture in sand and gravel, an archaeological dig for dolls. The works of humans are visible from the air because our machines make it possible to carve out large areas, erect large forms within the body and being of creation. My own being inside this mechanical marvel is large, exaggerated, significant in comparison with the minutiae below. And you, there in the distance beneath us, are little, scarcely noticed, of scant consideration.

We approach Penobscot Bay, the bumpy contour of Camden Hills to our right. A smokestack of the Bucksport paper mill—thin and white—the large green island of Verona, jewel in the throat of the great river. The small white side of Fort Knox comes into view as we pass Mt. Tuck.

Guidance from Augusta's VOR plays out. We still have the compass and begin looking for specific lakes—landmarks—to guide us. I stare at outlines upon the chart, look down out the window. So many lakes pass, pass away. One after the other beneath our stationary black wheel—and I lose track. How easy to be lost flying in air, to lose any airstrip upon the unfamiliar various beautiful land. And without that airstrip... where would we be? Will Deblois be lost?

Allen's voice tickles in my ear, in my earphones, startling me from reverie. *Pretty good wind drift right here. See how the plane goes off?* He gestures southward.

The wind!

Yet, even now at this tilting reminder I fail to grasp its significance for this flight, for me.

Bogs are appearing regularly below, bright green and oval, tapering. A dark river curls through green green bog. Now there are wide plains crisscrossed with beige lines—The blueberry barrens.

Then Allen sees it: the Deblois airstrip. He banks, descending to pattern altitude, but finds he must correct for the wind and do a straight approach. Sinking, I peer out on colorful moving specks and scattered piles of red upon the vast green. There are neat barracks-style blue camps in rows—now abandoned by law. Pickers are bused or drive out to the fields in their beat-up old cars over reams of rutty roads. There's a warehouse of the same blue hue and a company name, visible from the air.

A thump of turbulence. That old sinking feeling, this prickling thrill. The strip enlarges significantly as we descend. Jouncing.

And mockery moves in my mind as I recall my earlier desire to learn flight, to someday fly and land a plane. The field of tarmac expands like a balloon blown up in my face. I feel the rapid rate of descent and a stiff crosswind. The landing. It's certain: I will never land a plane, never land an airplane. I will never land a machine that flies through the air.

For all Allen's care, the landing is off-center. The light little 150 craft is routed by the crosswind. I have that old relief and dissipation of tremendous tension: We are down.

Pouring on prop power, Allen turns the plane and we begin back-taxiing toward 330. At the end of runway 330 is a dirt road through the green field, leading to pickers—and the blue outhouse, for my searching gaze. The Deblois airstrip, the blueberry corporation's own, is in the midst of a vast blueberry field.

Allen turns off the engine and we sit momentarily in sudden silence. It nudges the craft. It whistles under the wings. Wind. It speeds across the barrens with lonesome desolate force.

. . . *Uh-oh.* . . .

I'm numb from the long ride aloft in a vibrating machine. I reach, and manage to flip the latch, swing the door open. Out I climb, stiff. Together we start down the dirt path toward workers . . . and the privy. Allen stops to scoop a handful of blueberries. I keep walking toward the workers, toward the outhouse nearby them. Lining the path are those piles of red I saw from the air: plastic berry boxes.

Writing for the *Bangor Daily News*, Clayton Beal told of fluctuating and uncertain raker rates. Box prices vary year-to-year and are often not revealed until the workers are in the field. In 1986 the rate dropped 35 cents a box because they had picked an outstanding crop the year before. This is the reward of the diligent seasonal worker?

According to the Salt Center for Documentary Field Studies, harvests are accomplished by crews of 40 to 45 rakers who work for a leaseholder. Crews are Canadian and US Native Americans, and Mainers, local descendents of settlers. The latter eke out the livings of teachers, fisherman, clammers and loggers. Of the former, Micmacs, Malecites and Passamaquoddies all take part. When Europeans first landed and explored these barrens, they found the native peoples communally harvesting barrens in a prudent and proven manner.

It's morally estranging that these are the workers who go hungry before they feed you and me. Migrant workers, whose hard-working hands are so ready to feed us, depend on the indignity of handouts before they can begin work. The Good Shepard Food-Bank, a faithful make-do operation, knows about the problem in Maine. In a paper entitled *More Than Food*, I will soon be reading about red-tape bound General Assistance. The bureaucracy, which stands in our stead as taxpayer's steward, will neglect to provide for arriving workers because precise documentation is lacking. Rules change, labyrinthine paperwork fails, people who would feed us go hungry. All prior to the start of harvest. Here's a precise document: a hungry body and weary soul that is nonetheless eager to work. And this situation is that of agribusiness in general, usurping land that (morally) might be owned as familial and communal. As it once was: by the clan or family in the midst of a healthy *community*.

A man goes into the portable outhouse. I stand away, surveying this section of barrens, these locals, trying to take everything in. The minutiae as well as the vastness. A blonde woman straightens up from berry-raking. She moves stiffly toward a big old gas-guzzler parked by the privy.

I smile foolishly and say, "Hi!" What am I to these workers—someone who came down from the sky to use the privy? Someone with enough money to spare for a junket?

She fumbles with pieces of wet clothing laid out on a sheet of plastic on the trunk of her car. A twisted pair of panties falls into the dirt. "Goddamnit," she says. "At this rate I'll never get the laundry done." (Making a joke of it?)

The man steps down out of the portable privy and walks away. I move toward it, Allen having caught up with me is now also waiting to use it. When I come out, the blonde raker, her laundry, and the car, are gone, having sped off for parts unknown. Did I scare her away—or has she begun a fifteen or twenty mile torture trip over jolting gravel to find a dryer?

I watch a man and woman stooping over the task. They stoop to scoop, and turn, dumping berries into red containers. Stoop to scoop, and turn to dump. Stoop to scoop, and turn to dump. Continual stooping, stooping and turning. I begin to feel it in the back as I watch. While Allen takes his turn in the portable, I glean snippets of conversation from the two rakers, finding myself too shy to approach and ask nosy occupational questions.

The woman says something about stiffness and ointment.

"I'm about Ben-Gayed out," returns the man. He wears shorts, a bandanna and has a long bushy beard. The sweeping wind makes it hard to catch every word. Then ". . . some strange man crawling into bed with you." He laughs.

I grimace. Why is it I just don't like talk that robs lovemaking of its beautiful appeal: words which bring sex down into the dirt instead of raising it up on the cool stems of orchids or lady slippers (which, however, spring from the dirt)? The man has a beautiful form—tan and fit from his labor among the fruit. The fruit he picks is shapely, sweet, a pulpy container of seed and emblem of ripeness and sexuality. He works mechanically, ten back-breaking hours a day in the sun on a barren full of fruit, the result of sexual reproduction. Because of the monotony of his repetitious action and industrial proportions of the work, he must see and feel his hand scooping blueberries all night long. The days are spent turning blue fruit into green currency, the source of his living throughout the month of August.

Perhaps the fortunes of these workers will change when the mechanical harvesters overrun the barrens. The world's largest harvester (at this writing) is a steel monster, 16 ft. wide and 20 ft. high, with 700 rakes mounted on belts. Three years ago, in 1987, it was picking 1000 boxes a day with the aid of four people. When the machine ousts them, migrants will be further cut off from the land, inexorably losing their connectedness with the source of their bodies, the soil. This blue fruit of beauty in its green bed is the mediator of life between them (and us) and the soil. Ten hours a day, a paying fruit and a broken back are better than absence, machinery, and no pay. The best is to own the land you tend, the fruit you pick for your family. Familial and communally, yours.

Allen joins me and we turn to walk back toward the plane. Is it absurd to hire a plane and fly—clumsy, mechanical, noisy, polluting, and anxious—across the state? To a county at the opposite end, get out, go to the toilet, hear a snatch of conversation out of context, grab a handful of fruit and fly away? Is it absurd and fantastic? *Ayuh.*

Walking, I reach down into the low berry-laden bushes for the guilty handful. The practically rainless July has our Department of Agriculture thinking the season's harvest will be half what it was last year, but this patch is burgeoning. There appear to be two kinds of berries, two shades of blue. One is dark, purplish, reminiscent of grapes; the other a light blue, like pale dense sky. The Cherryfield-Narraguagus Historical Society sent me a packet containing essays for a contest they sponsored. Eighth-grade essayist Renee Foss of Harrington wrote about types of lowbush berries. Some are prone to disease, causing crop loss. One is a fungus attacking the blossoms when weather is cool and wet. Other diseases include witches broom, redleaf, leaf rust, powdery mildew. The variety within the Maine wild blueberry makes for resistance. Resistance not found in the uniform. It is part of the elegant mechanism of nature, of her complex tapestry of land races, the enduring various species.

I crush the thieving handful between my teeth and juice pours over my gums and down my parched throat. How dry and tight my throat has been, how refreshing and necessary the taste of blueberries just now. I long to sit down and eat, to feed among the berries, but they aren't ours, and there is another pilot waiting his turn with the plane at the Oxford Airport.

I grab onto a wing strut and fit myself into the cockpit. The plane rocks and creaks in the wind.

. . . *Uh-oh.* . . . The little answering quiver wakes in me.

We bank away above the barrens and I look northward toward a stark geometrical plot of rich brown earth. It's scored with darker lines and limned with white. Trenches and piping? At one end is a clean white structure with three silos. Children's toys. Where's the organic in the articles below? If I were down on the ground with them I'd have a sense of their lack of proportion. Are gigantic boxes, cylinders, networks of pipes necessary to our nourishment? By monstrous mechanical harvesters? Does it reinforce the deceptive view that production of food with hands is solely drudging and joyless? But hunter-gatherers knew. There is no joy below me in a plot at once immense, artificial, technological. But how about stooping-and-turning, ten hours a day? I'm a domestic, and a creative writer—arrogantly I raise questions. I just don't answer them.

We cross above a jewel-like green bog, teardrop in shape, surrounded in dark conifer. Now our tail is toward morning sun. I see our formerly trailing shadow-craft ahead of us, moving over the green Ground of Maine.

Occasional turbulence, *thump!* Our elevation is 2600 ft., our guide a magnetic compass: heading due west.

Visiting the Eastern Uplands

Feel the RPM's pick up going into this wind? Allen's voice tickles through the radio headphones clamped over my ears. He gives it more throttle and says we'll ascend to 3000 ft. where it should be a bit smoother. I smile and touch his arm in gratitude.

My ears begin popping as we climb. The headphones cut some of the swishing, droning and consuming noise of the mechanical craft, but they carry an electrical droning of their own. A constant low static and occasional rhythmic buzzing. Sometimes I'm pierced by the ablated disembodied voices of other traffic.

He tells me to find a landmark due west and he'll fly for it. After a bit I spy the thin spewing stack at Bucksport, and point. He looks over at me, grins. Maybe he's enjoying the look on my face. He says, *It's your turn to fly.*

The plan to ascend has brought scant respite from the occasional *thump-bam!* Western skies are gathering their morning's allotment of low level ozone and haze. The air over there is dirty and we are heading for it. A heavy line blankets the horizon, reaches toward the north and mountains in a vague dirty blue distance. These gases come up from the country's great mechanized Northeast Corridor. They are one of the indicators of turbulence and must be scaled if we are to escape it. Worse, before this runs a broken and clotting raft of cumulus toward which we're progressing. Above that line we would perhaps find calm air. But it's probably too high for the Cessna 150. That ominous retribution of industrialization is just too steep for our little craft.

Greenhouse gases, but one of corporate America's apparently lasting legacy to our children's children, are what Senator George Mitchell called "the man who came to dinner": they'll stay and stay. The Senate majority leader from Maine wrote in his book *World on Fire* that CO_2 emissions may stay up there for centuries. They are being released far faster than the atmosphere can remove them. Were we to keep emitting them at current levels they will intensify up there, indefinitely.

In trying to stay his course into the wind, Allen's arm and grip are tiring. He takes his hands from the yoke and jokes about flying with the rudder pedals. *Might find some clean air a bit higher . . . We'll try 4500 ft.* We are crossing the Penobscot, passing the paper mill with its smokestack below.

Fumble in my purse for a motion sickness tablet. Have forgotten to bring something to wash it down. The tiny white pill breaks between my teeth. Clouds pass quickly, flowing eastward on the wind like scum upon a river. We drone westward through the flow, pushing through currents. The wind pushes back, hard, requiring yet more fuel. *Whump. Bang!* The tablet, disintegrating in my mouth, bites back with a bitter taste as its protective coating melts away and begins burning the tip of my tongue. An acrid chemical burning. *Bang!*

I'm trying to take notes, hoping for occupation to settle my unhappy mind. Below I see some small circular bog overtaking a wooded area. Dead trees have fallen there like pickup sticks on a carpet of green. Who can pick up a stick without disturbing the others? Can any of the children who play with these toys? My mouth is on fire. My inner cheeks and gums burn. The tip of my tongue turns numb.

Clouds roll over us, one by one. Updrafts below lift and jolt us as we pass under them. Allen ascends to 5500 ft., then 5800 ft.. Man-made things below shrink to insignificance. And I can heed them no more. The immanent dirty elements are all. Cloud, wind and gravity's threat have consorted to pound the pomposity, along with its imagined securities, from my puny soul.

(With good luck, it says, you'll never have severe turbulence.) Enfeebled, I look above toward the blue.

There's the pallid moon ahead! waning before midday. It is reclining, belly-up, and sickly pale. I take off the headphones so Allen won't hear me murmuring psalms. It's so noisy I can feel the words vibrating in my larynx but the sound of them never reaches my ears. Now I am letting-go the controls (as advised), hoping the craft of my own being will right itself. *Bang! Bang! Bang!* A thousand fears crowd into my mind. I thrust them back with inaudible recitation. Below me the Maine Corridor, our humble extension of the great Northeast Corridor (commercial, industrial, political) is spread out beneath the dingy air. (*I will fear no evil. . . .*)

Allen looks over at me, concerned. He asks if I want him to land below at Augusta. It's a sacrificial offering. He would have to leave me and fly on to Oxford then drive maybe 60 miles through the hills to pick me up in the car. Mutely, I shake my head.

Having passed the Kennebec, we begin descending over Androscoggin and then Oxford counties. The toy villages, so peaceful, serene enlarge. One in particular catches my eye, Hebron, with its Academy—recognizable by the graceful lawn surrounded in stately brown buildings, the neat small edifices of learning—now on vacation. We round the green mound, Little Singepole Mountain, which rises above it, comforting rock. Beside it hunkers Streakéd Mountain.

I spy the automotive raceway—a landmark—beside which the runway spreads. The airport runway that never looked so blessed. Never have I so longed for landing. Give me to drink of its nausea and despair. Increase the sickness and sinking of this jolting descent. Fill my mind with all its attendant and frantic fears. Let me drink to the last drop these necessary dregs . . . for when it is drunk we will be *down*.

Oh, the welcome expanding tarmac, the veering and hopping of our quaking craft.

Ah Allen, Allen, we've landed! We are down from the turbulent sky!

I tried to negotiate the aisles at the Oxford Hills grocery store but kept veering slightly right; pushing the cart. Disoriented.

"I feel like I'm crabbing into the wind," I said to Allen beside me.

"It's how I held the yoke all the way back." He rubbed his shoulder. "I must've pulled a tendon or something, trying to keep it on course."

It was that northeast flowing river of wind, that struggle with windshear, gusts and convection. He flew a heading of 330° in order to maintain a course of 270°, because the wind kept forcing us off course.

"That flight tested all my skills—control, communication, navigation. The wind clipped so much off our speed I thought we were flying backward."

When we stepped from the store into the parking lot, I looked up, seeing soft cumulus overhead, interstitial with the calm blue sky. Those clouds adrift there, so peaceful, serene. Now that we are no longer among them.

Life in the Highlands, Where Pipers Call

THE PIPER STANDS PLAYING beneath a tree by an entrance to the grounds. He plays a Gaelic air, leaving no doubt that we have arrived at the place and time: Highland Games downeast by the sea, presented by St. Andrew Society of Maine. The Society's purpose, to preserve and promote Scottish heritage, has brought folk from dozens of clans in New England and Nova Scotia to participate in the pipe and dance competitions.

Allen and I have no Scots ancestry that we are aware of (although some of my forebears were Celtic); nevertheless we're interested enough in this culture to come and experience the Maine Highland Games. I'm hungry for an authentic taste of scones, famous Scottish quick bread.

We walk down toward the lawn where a Border Collie demonstration is in progress. A haunting skirl of bagpipes floats to us on the breeze. The song will inform our awareness—now quiet and distant, now strong and near—throughout the day of these competitions. We join spectators ringing the fence where a small black dog with white markings chases shorthaired sheep. In the midst stands a tiny slat pen where the shepherdess stands, long bright ribbon from her hand tethering a gate of this pen. Shrilling, her small silver whistle pipes out a song of degrees—signals for the dog. The Border Collie runs this way and that as the shepherdess peeps and shrills, funneling sheep in the manner commanded by these high-pitched sounds.

The Collie drives them close against the fence under our noses. Furious breathing of these small cloven-hoofed woolly creatures fans our knees in passing. Now the song (with its various peeping) sounds again, the dog comes round driving them off the fence.

The Collie's ears are pricked; its long-haired coat sleek and glossy-looking as though brushed with care, but its stance reveals sentience, and intent of the rangiest predator. Agile, it scurries with head low and poised, alert to the whistle or words of the shepherdess who often commands the

Visiting the Eastern Uplands

dog to "lie down!" At this command the dog drops to its belly, crouched, ready to scramble at the next signal. Then, tearing the ground, it comes round and we feel the predatory power as its nails grip the turf. The dog pivots. Its breath is quick, excited. It spins away, cutting out two sheep, herding them into the slat pen. At once the handler closes the gate and loops the pink tether over its posts.

This green stifling lawn beneath shore pines is a far cry from the rugged and rolling distances of the Scottish Highlands where such sheep roam. There the dogs are signaled over vast distances, handily moving the woolbearers while a shepherd stands his or her ground. In this heat today I sense the discomfort of these beautiful sheep in the hurly of being so gathered, so harassed.

"Why do sheep run from the dog?" Someone has asked from the sidelines. Answer: It is a primordial response from an age when predators roamed the hills in packs. The quick would run the sheep silly then head them back toward slower pack members. There jaws would powerfully tear them to shreds, sustenance for hungry wolves. Sheep are still highly sensitive to the born predator who, through breeding and training, has become their guard and now serves for their good. Through the healthy instinct of fear.

Wandering away we follow the path past a competition ground. Here strong muscular men toss the camber. Shotput and tossing-the-sheaf are also powerfully executed. It's a contrast to the adjacent domestic camp of six or eight white canvas tents with canopy and fire pit. Smoke billows up on the breeze: smoke of buckwheat scorching on the griddle. Women are clustered in homespun gowns, petticoats, and linen headdresses—preparing food. Allen and I wander on, looking about at curiously attired folk, including children, who are dressed in the tartan of another time and an older culture not our own.

We come up toward the parade ground, neatly compassed by a ring of pavilions and concessions. There's a big old double-decker bus (blazoned with a Union Jack) that has been converted to a fish-n-chips stand. (We note its enclosed top deck with curtains, hints of homey furnishings in the windows—converted living quarters?) There are concessions for meat pies and bridies, for shish kebabs and sausages and buns, for rich and unScottish-looking desserts. A sign promises scones, but, when I receive one from

Allen where I sit in the shade, it turns out to be strawberry shortcake with whipped cream, thawed syrupy strawberries, and costing four dollars!

Other concessionaires sell faces carved in walking sticks. Some sticks are long and peeled, cedar sticks still covered in ragged bark. A face is carved in each, complete with crows feet round the eyes, representing ancient mythological protectors of the forest. Booths sell true woolens, tartans, weaving, glengarries, and cotton runners with homespun mottoes. Here's a plastic-covered carryall decorated with thistles: petaled purple heads with great prickly ovaries. At the bottom of the bag is a warning—and a welcome. I had been trying to recall the significance of the thistle and now it's written here in purple before my eyes. Complete with ugly coating of petroleum-based plastic, one of the wonders-run-amuck of our age.

I read somewhere recently that the molecular structure of plastic, a polymer, has been reproduced *organically*. A good thing, that? Saves petroleum for energy? Ordinary potatoes can be made to yield plastic grains in place of starch grains. The resultant tuber would contain polymers but still look like a potato. It wouldn't taste or nourish like one but provide a renewable source of plastic plates. Before the organic polymer-potato is commercially sown, some of the bugs will have to be worked out. Things like the inadvertent assimilation of the world's potato crop, evoking the cataclysm of Kurt Vonnegut's Ice-9 in *Cat's Cradle*. Bees are disinclined to distinguish between polymer potato blooms and starch potato blooms, thus potentially converting whole fields of food into fields of tubular plastic. Who knows what we'll have at our disposal with more tweaking of our scientific genius? Soon we'll be growing wax fruit to fill bowls on our coffee tables.

The words on this plastic-coated bag tell of the thistle tradition and its motto. Gardeners, bird-lovers and landscapers may admire the rich coloring of this flower but thistles are elsewhere considered a nuisance and covering of waste places, fit to be yanked and discarded. The motto before me in Latin reads: *"Nemo me impune laccessit"*. That is, "No one provokes me with impunity." Or, more fittingly, *"Wha duar meddle wi me."* A not inappropriate motto for this prickly plant which is honored for its aid in defeating eighth century Danish raiders. The barefoot invaders' stealthy nighttime approach was thwarted when thistles growing about the camp brought forth such cries of pain that the sleeping Scots were alerted. It has since been an emblem of guardianship.

Nemo me impune laccessit is a warning whose power to convince is contingent upon the power of the speaker. It's what renders the motto believable. Today with our glib high-tech weaponry we might find threats of sword and broadaxe borne on bare feet ridiculous or romantic. They belong to an age when every man was a warrior that he might protect his family, community, land. But given the might of our contemporary weaponry we must go beyond the wielding of known armaments to find a speaker worthy enough to fear. We must think big, *really* big—of prodigiously polluted earth, of mighty yet intricate ecosystems unbalanced, of the once-kindly atmosphere now filled with mountains of carbon, of ultraviolet radiation pouring down on flesh. Think of great Nature when Nature is wronged.

Out of a blue and white pavilion comes the melancholy song of the folk singer. He sings of a berm beside a loch where a young woman stood, long ago . . . bereft but sensing the loving presence of her lost young man. Now the music changes. The singer yields up a rousing song of the Shakers who danced and quaked—to the glory of God. "I am the Lord of the Dance, sang he—dance, dance, whatever ye may be."

Allen and I move on for our own dance of sorts: a walk along the pitched row where each clan presents its genealogy: names like Kincaid MacBean MacPherson MacThomas Moffat, Hannah and Scot. Names moving with substance inside the mouth. Names to stick a bit in the throat and curl the tongue as they pass out to the listening ear. A roll call of clans, sons of the ancients, whose system dominated Scotland for nearly 700 years. According to *The Clans and Tartans of Scotland* by Robert Bain, chiefs of these clans took their oaths standing, with both feet upon a stone, promising to preserve the ancient ways. Chanting the noble exploits of their forebears, bards exhorted clan members to "emulate" the example of its past.

Hot asphalt curves round the parade ground and we follow beyond genealogical booths, feeling the heat of this fiery path through the soles of our 20th-century shoes. Here are booths for the handiwork of a bygone age. I can't help but stop to stare. On the table before me is a fabric of chains. Heavy fabric of metal-work, pieced together a ring at a time. This, then, is chain mail. I slip out a hand, touching it.

A man in ancient garb stands by, ready to instruct us. He takes two tiny rings and spreads one open with pliers, hooks it to another, pinches it closed and picks up a third. This mesh of three is in turn hooked to a fourth. Dimension develops, thickness, like that of the mail lying before me. He knits protection, a quarter-inch ring at a time. I am absorbed, watching his hands.

Life in the Highlands, Where Pipers Call

Also receiving instruction is a sweating and heavily bearded man struggling into some thigh-length chain mail, weighing about thirty pounds. Its maker guides him through a method of donning and doffing. He then tells of the hardy primitive Highlanders who fought naked because they felt forged protection slowed a fighter, robbing him of agility. He offers me chain mail to try on. Grinning I decline.

Now he shows us weaponry. Great two-handed claymores, capable of cleaving plate armor. Round wooden shields were covered in hide and held in place by a pattern of stud-works strapped to the arm; and hidden beneath, a dirk, tightly clenched in the hand of the warrior. Our guide slides a wide double-edged sword from its sheath—crossed-shaped forged steel with blood-gutter running to its hilt.

Allen and I are turned about by the song of approaching pipers. Here come marchers in kilts with staves, standards flapping. Near the head of the parade march our friends, Blaine and Margaret (MacBean), our town historian and his wife. The men wear swinging kilts, sporrans, and glengarries, followed by a multitude of young women pipers in swaying red tartan skirts. Their fingers fly upon chanters, their bright cheeks expel breath into the reed. Elbows pump hard against the bag at their ribs. Sweat soaks them. The skirling and droning pours upon me with the day's heat like ravishing ointment, setting up a quiver along my sensory pathways toward the person within.

As the bands pass in color and sound, I look over my shoulder to see bearded men at the chain mail booths donning their barbaric gear: helms, battle-axes, arm shields, spears, swords. Some are mantled in animal skin, some skirted and draped in nine yards of tartan. They step off cool turf onto scorching asphalt in bare feet, nothing flinching, and join the parade.

"Look at that!"

But Allen laughs: "They're warriors, aren't they?"

It's a searing summer day. Sun fires down, burning the top of my bare head as we wait in the gathering. Watching and still, crowds compass the parade ground where Highland bands assemble for the opening ceremony of The Games. I done my floppy white hat, stuff my hair under it, relieved at once by cessation of burning. Standing here in the penetrating fire, I can't help but think of the hole in the high ozone layer . . . especially its dissipation in these higher latitudes where the crown of Maine juts into Canada.

Visiting the Eastern Uplands

Inert gases produced by the wonders of our age—refrigeration, the space shuttle, aerosols and Styrofoam—ascend to the stratosphere, gobbling up protective ozone by molecular conversion. The great bright hole in the sky pours out radiation, that mighty mutagen, off-cast of our sun's fusion. Mutagens transform genetic material of skin tissue by changing the sequence of nucleotides in its DNA. Instructions for healthy cell formation are changed into instructions for disease. For every 2% reduction of protective ozone, there is an estimated 10% increase in skin cancers.

Standing here, listening but seeing little of the pipers because of the press in this sweaty gathering, I notice a young man in front of me wearing a faded T-shirt with motto: *the cure/the prayer*, in black letters on a pattern of faded foliage. I continue to stare at it as the pipes drone, sensing some metaphoric significance . . . but then the moment passes, its meaning gone with it. Signs and symbols strike upon the intellect, engaging it briefly and darting away. Or they live on breathless, bemused. Did I really see something in my anxiety—or is it just an old shirt?

But I can take this burning no longer. Agreeing, Allen and I break from the crowd and plunge toward the shade of the pines. Here we find ongoing dance competitions in progress and sit down to watch from an out-of-the-way bench. It's harder to see the dancers from our oblique position but we must stay out of the sun. I am relieved by the cool grace of the offshore breeze.

Three little ones dance on the sheltering wooden stage, leaping like sprites. One-legged, toes pointed, each wee dancer reaches a poised hand on high as though in refined praise. The skirling and droning of a lone piper helps them, and they are light and finely formed in their pleats, argyles and laced up slippers. White puffy sleeves, lacy ascots and velvet vests complete the lassies' outfits. The little legs kick back, the arms akimbo. They pivot, they leap, they dance dance dance. The piper, who pipes obscurely in a rear corner of the stage, is also a marvel. I recall Blaine telling me about the piper who played incessantly from nine in the morning till six at night for the competitions last year. He emphasized the quality of this feat in saying that the bag must continue *full of breath*.

I look now toward the open field before the stage where a lone judge sits. She is raised to an elevated position by a canvas chair set high on a picnic table. On her lap rests a clipboard. She watches and writes as dancers in groups of three perform the hornpipe before her critical gaze. The

Life in the Highlands, Where Pipers Call

diminutive dancers begin and end each dance with a bow to her. Grace. The music beats faster and faster but the judge, wearing a yellow sun dress with spaghetti straps, sits still in the burning sun as they leap.

I begin to marvel more at the judge than the dancers who are shaded and sheltered. Later, as I roam the grounds while the day wears, I will marvel still more. For whenever I look in the direction of the dancers there will be the judge . . . watching and writing, seated, as though for eternity, in the fiery sun.

Rested, we stand and make our way past dancers down toward the white tents of domestic encampment which we passed on our way to the parade ground earlier. Approaching, I hear a young woman telling a few listeners about historical roles. They are camp followers, respected young women chosen by lottery to follow the Highland soldiers. They prepare foods such as scones on the griddle. They wash linens and care for the children they bring.

I sense movement at my feet and look down. There is a sweet babe, in a long white gown, sitting in a wooden tub draped in wool. She looks up at me with direct trusting blue eyes and a wet smile. The babe sucks on a smooth wooden orb held in her dimpled hand. And as she sucks, she hums. Her humming is dulcet and dreamy although she smiles at me with true awareness in her heaven's eyes. It is long before I look away.

Beside her is another tub toward which she leans, dropping her orb. The tub holds a few inches of water afloat with smooth wood-turnings of various shapes. The babe reaches down and splashes the water, watching the turnings bob in its ripples. Then she picks out a spindle and begins gumming it. The young woman working at the table notices my interest and tells me the baby's name is Kelsey.

I step over to watch the women's preparation of food, and to ask questions about their attire. Now I see genuine scones heaped in a steaming plateful. Some are scorched from the iron griddle. Scones look like triangular buckwheat biscuits, homely, not high or light. Does the word derive from the place called Scone, where the Stone of Destiny became the coronation stone in 843 A.D.? Or is it the other way around? Websters says that the word comes from the Dutch *schoonbrood*, meaning pure clean bread.

On the women's table are crockery, stone jugs and pewter tankards. On their heads are long white scarves with folds binding their crowns. The linen is held in place with a neat gold pin in the midst of the head.

Visiting the Eastern Uplands

Historically, the scarves indicated that the women were married. The cloths were treasured for this, says the baby's mother. Beneath the gowns and petticoats they wore linen shifts in which they slept. Linen was considered precious, probably because being homespun and woven of homegrown flax it was difficult to make. The top of one bodice is held in place by a three-inch black thorn. She tells me this is a hawthorn, from a hawthorn tree. It is authentic as part of the camp follower's dress: fierce, like the spirit of a camp follower. As with the thistle, this three-inch black thorn epitomizes this life in the Highlands, where pipers call. "*Wha duar meddle wi me?*"

Down the facing rows of white tents are highland soldiers from the time of bonnie Prince Charlie: their garb is not ancient—no chain mail here. They wear tartans, carry flintlock muskets and swords with basket hilts. One soldier gives us a demonstration on the proper loading and firing of the flintlock using shot, powder, ramrod and pan. Wearing maybe six yards of tartan, he shows how the clansmen pleated their long tartans on belts— belted long or short, depending on the terrain and weather. The leftover length was used as a cloak during cold weather, as hooded cloak when it rained, or it could be slung over a shoulder out of the way and fastened with a brooch. The whole thing could be used as a blanket when sleeping on the ground. Six yards of wool was the rule, and the saying, "the whole nine yards" originated with that particular length.

In *The Clans and Tartans of Scotland*, Robert Bain writes that the original tartans were dyed with indigenous plants of the various regions of the Highlands and Western Islands. They were woven in simple check patterns. Folk, and the regions of their birth, were identified by indigenous colors and patterns of the tartan they wore. These patterns were carefully preserved by town weavers, who kept wooden sticks with numbered threads for each tartan they wove.

So strong was the meaning of each pattern to its wearer that these became patriotic emblems, eventually provoking their English overlords to outlaw the wearing of tartan by an Act of Parliament. The tactic to defeat this tradition worked because forty years later, when the Act was repealed, there was little interest on the part of the new generation. Knowledge of the correct identifying patterns was lost in the intervening years. It took the interest of Britain's George IV to reawaken tartan joy in Highlanders. In 1822, nearly 80 years after the prohibition of patterns, the King's visit to lowland Edinburgh brought a revival of traditional dress. Patterns used were largely recent creations, however.

Allen hefts the musket held out to him. The soldier talks on about fighting methods of the Regiment. A glimmer of reflected light from nearby shadows captures my eye. In the shade of nestling pines I spy baby Kelsey at her mother's breast: a picture of nurturing grace, yielding forth a quiet spirit.

Allen and I walk to the shore. The tide comes rippling in. We watch spartina grass, bent in the breeze. The view here opens out between long arms of shore, hinting of open sea beyond. An offshore breeze blows upon us, as though a base drone, with smaller fitful gusts as of tenor pipes. The mighty concert of Nature, sun, sea, and shore, all consort to orchestrate these convection currents. I think of the breath of the Piper, whose playing coaxes the Dance. Somewhere behind us, distantly, haunting skirls of the bag, chanter and drone, drift back to us. Through this sounding wind.

Departure

A PALE MORNING OUTSIDE the window. Light just beginning to show among green leaves. I sat in bed, sipping coffee and reading the fiery *Book of Ezekiel*. A few days before I had read about the departure of the Glory of God from Jerusalem. Now the prophet was carried in a vision to the New Gate where stood the house of God remade. Looking eastward he saw the Glory of God returning, descending toward him and toward that new temple. "And his voice is like a noise of many waters, and the earth shined with his glory." Is such radiance after all a feminine attribute, as the *Shekinah*, the settling of God, has been described?

I looked up from the old words and tried to visualize a sight I would see from the top of Deer Hill Road. I wondered if I might glimpse in some sort what Ezekiel saw . . . if I were perched up there as the sun ascended. Would the green land of hills, and the valley of ponds, be glorified by golden light as the heavenly fire passed on high? Could I gain there a sense of the approximate and feminine Glory of God?

I donned my floppy white hat to keep deer flies off my head, and opened the front door. Then I pushed the bike out, careful to make no sound—did not want to wake the dark old dog, sleeping on trampled and barren dirt, where I had tethered him.

I looked up. One long cloud was moving to diffuse and cover a golden-white sun above the wall of woods edging my neighbor's yard. A day moving toward the perfection of its shining? Or were clouds on the increase to obscure?

The climbing stretch of hill-country road passed quickly beneath the patterned wheels as I manipulated the multiple gears of the bicycle. This middle-aged strength was fresh in my legs. Roadside things passed in glimpses—laden blackberry bushes in the curve; red limp freshly

Departure

spray-poisoned dwarf sumac beneath the power lines; a bright sporty car tucked among trees. Feeling sweat flow now, I switchbacked on the steep grade before the big u-shaped house on the flat stretch. Here I passed clots of flowering virgin's bower, a three-leafed vine mistaken for poison ivy upon our first moving to Maine.

Passing the big house of the Scot, I looked out toward the folds of old hills. Mists lay thickly in those valleys, but it did not shine. The murk of polluted sky with further mountains shadowed from the light. Vapors below met those above in heavy diffusion.

Fireweed, tall and tapering, lit the road shoulders. Now I rolled rapidly down dirt-and-gravel where the road dips before it climbs higher. In damp sand I saw the cloven imprint of the deer, but held on course, steering with care on a sloppy and uncertain surface.

There was Mr. Kaplan's old connected dwelling, neat as a needle. Across the road was an old stone wall. Here country-cultivated shrubs had grown large and rugged among wildflowers and weeds. Here was a view of empty distance and thickening sky.

The hill ascended steepest here and breathing was heavy, weighted with the oppressive atmosphere. I pushed the damp hat back off my forehead, then found myself off the bike, absently pushing it up hill, switching back, as I had done when peddling. Breathless and sticky, I came to an end of the road proper and looked up a scrubby slope toward hidden moldering old gravestones, spied worn steps among the overgrowth—made of decaying railroad ties. I pulled the bike off road into the bushy birch thickets, climbed to the stone wall. Soon I was seated on cushiony lichen, soft covering of old stone.

Now I looked up toward the great bright globe of gas, the ancient physical source of all we have here. It was hidden among clouds of subtlest gray, but the blessed light of shining pressed through in subdued glory. An elliptical ring of it pierced the cloud roundabout.

I looked toward the valley of ponds but the view was obscured by leafy trees. Yet I saw Swans Ridge out there, elevated above a ravine. A gash below lines of conifer declared the saw of the logger, who had cut the lush covering of Swans Ridge for a developer. There was evidence of that road to Swans Ledge, which I had explored in the spring with the neighbor girls, rising away on my right. Directly across the road from me, ravaged foliage of dwindling summer held on in thick muggy air. Crickets, harbinger of season's end, chirruped steadily in bushes roundabout, and opposite me a chickadee squeaked. Now heavy silence.

The cloud above Swans was darkening. In vapor above the gashed ridge an elliptical shaping of light slowly overwhelmed the ridge. Diminishing, it seeped out in vague crepuscular rays.

What is the saddest account in the whole of the *Old Testament*? Is it not that of the departure of the *Shekinah* from the Holy of Holies? Departure of the Glory from Jerusalem, the city of peace, itself? "Then the glory of the Lord went up from the cherub, and stood over the threshold of the house; and the house was filled with cloud, and the court was full of the brightness of the Lord's glory."

That was the same house that the worshipers had been polluting. They had also polluted the high places roundabout Jerusalem. "And the glory of the Lord went up from the midst of the city and stood upon the mountain which is on the east side of the city."

The story which follows, of Jerusalem's destruction, is one of the most powerful tragedies ever told and, with the exception of Holocaust, and current ongoing Holocaust of today's Ethnic Cleansing, is perhaps the saddest.

The sky above Swans Ridge, indeed the whole atmosphere over the valley of ponds, was dirty with cloud. The crepuscular rays were gone now. Only a dull crack, the suggestion of light, remained. The sun had vanished.

I stood up and started through brush toward the rotting railroad-ties, leading down to the road.

As I went, spreading humble lowbush blueberries—tiny, pale and blue—invited. I bent down and plucked a meager handful. So good and sweet, so wild. I pulled the bike out of young saplings and turned onto the road.

Gliding down the steep hill past Kaplan's, I felt my hat slipping off by degrees as the wind of my flight tore it. Off it flew, a wild white thing. I reached for it with my right hand. The left pulled impulsively at the brake. The bike stopped dead and I tumbled over its handlebars, careening into the dirt and pain of my fall.

I was scraped and banged—*stung*! Caked in dirt, I climbed unsteadily to my feet and, shaking, brushed off my jeans, my blouse and arms. I picked up the bike, straightened the brake holds and handlebars.

Peddling down, then once again back along the flat, I saw tall thickets of brown bitterdock that I had not noticed on the way up. They spired like

Departure

drought-burnt flame: their leaves drying red from lack of moisture and seasonal lessening of light. Nearing the big house of the Scot, I looked out toward the mountains, now heavily shrouded.

It would have to be another day—to approximate the Glory of God.

Future Maine

I'M IN THE BEDROOM upstairs, sitting at the old oak kitchen table, now my desk. It's where I write words of warning. I am a writer, and that is what writers do. They comment on life. (It's no longer called moralizing—old-fashioned word.) Comment: there is a bridge out—midway—on the route along which we roar.

But I'm not really thinking of that at the moment because my fingers are sifting through thistle seeds. My eyes stare unseeing out the window into the backyard and beyond, into the logged-over woods. Unseeing, because I'm concentrating on messages tactile, not visual.

The seeds feel minute. They feel the size of salt grains, but I know they're larger because I looked at them. Rubbing the grains between my thumb and fingers or just covering my palms with them, sifting, I feel natural oils from these seeds.

I found the seeds when we were on our way back from Portland, where Allen had been doing genealogical research at the library. Wedged between the car door and passenger seat where I rode—a genuine thistle with three blossoms in different stages, budding, blooming, and gone-by. We found them below the Eastern Promenade. Something big had squashed a four-feet thicket of them, leaving pale canes radiating a spiny green-and-lavender crown of leaves and blooms. I continued to think of it, trying to guess what felled them (as though some large body had flown through the night willy-nilly and landed thus unhappily). We remained mystified. It did however remind us of the Scottish heritage of the thistle. Thistles that once alerted the Scots to the presence of enemies. The motto which goes with the emblem: *Nemo me impune laccessit. No one provokes me with impunity.*

Our plucked thistles rode with us in an aluminum can full of water where I had tucked them out-of-the-way so they wouldn't pierce my skin with their fierce spines. (Why, by the way, do we fuss with plastic and aluminum containers? Do we know how much energy it takes to recycle them into new containers—which are promptly drained and again in need of recycling? As Allen suggests from time to time, "Why not use returnable glass containers? It takes far less energy to clean glass than it does to make new containers." And think of the new and local business for it. This is how it was done in the days when soda bottles were shapely and I carried an ugly leather black bucket purse.)

We were passing into Gray, Maine when I noticed a sign proclaiming thistle seeds for sale in front of a sprawling lawn-and-garden store. My ignorance was so great that I cried out. "Allen, stop! I want to know why thistle seeds are sold." Could not picture a gardener planting such seeds, not even a Scottish gardener. Once inside I was told that songbirds love them. So, with a sackful, I left the jolly clutter of the greenhouse-cum-lawnchair-whirligigs-shop.

The seeds in the bag are black. Seated at the oak table, I take a tiny hundred in my palm to examine. They remind me of mouse turds—narrow and curved, larger at one end than the other. Under the aspheric magnifier they bloom large, and show three sides with striations lengthwise. They are markedly different from the seeds of the bull thistle that Allen cut for me from the Portland thicket below the Promenade.

Sharp prickles are everywhere on this plant. Gingerly I lift the cutting from the aluminum can. Its leaves, green calyx, and stem are all thick with spines, an identifying feature of the bull thistle. Only the lavender petal parts, thickly coated with white pollen, are soft and velvety to the touch.

I leave this flower intact, but pull the dried brown petal parts of a gone-by bloom. They come forth in a multitude. Below these parts, inside the spiny ovary, are myriad pale seeds attached to folded dandelion-like carriers. I pull gently, drawing these forth into a feathery pile. A breeze from the open window blows on them and slowly they open and pop up in a cottony heap, poised to waft about the room.

Quickly I quash the bagful of black seeds down on the living, burgeoning pile. A few feathery puffs escape and blow across the table.

I take some, parting them from the feather carriers and hold them, glistening, in my palm. Now I examine them with the magnifier and add a few black seeds for comparison. The black ones are longer, more narrow at one end. *Newcombe's* shows several species. There's even a yellow one instead of lavender.

The cutting is several days old now. It's been that long since we came back from Portland. I run my fingers thoughtfully along the grain of the spines. It seems that the older and dryer a plant becomes, the less piercing it grows to the touch.

I have filled and hung my feeder. The songbirds may show anytime. When I toted a bucket purse in junior high, Rachel Carson's *Silent Spring* came out, causing a worthy stir. It showed the significance of songbirds as environmental indicators.

Here the woods surrounding our house on two sides have been thinned considerably, causing me to wonder about the wood thrush and veery. How will they find it for seclusion and breeding in coming years? Thanks to Carson, NIMBY (Not in My Backyard) has become a worthy acronym. I don't denigrate it: There are no backyard stewards but ourselves. It may be the closest we come to holding our spiritual ground in the physical realm.

This morning, one of those stifling dirty days, I walked up the road with the dog, picking blackberries. We left the road when we got to the powerline where dwarf sumac had been poisoned by herbicide, standing stiff, brown and dried like statues of dead trees. Here one sees the wide brutal path of the skidder intersecting the powerline's swath.

I stepped into that swath then turned down into blasted woodland. It'd been a few weeks since we heard the roar and clank of the skidder moving in woods behind our house. The living-wage work of the logger was done. Now might be a good time to bushwhack back through the forest and see what the saw had done.

Maine has had a strange geo-history, written in earth (rock and soil) over millions of years, but the strangest may be yet to come. And this strangeness would stem from the speed with which changes occurred. They would not be written in earth so much as in atmosphere, another ancient controlling element of our life. No, the changes of the past were not small, but slow. Vast changes, both mighty and megalithic. Question: In geo-historical terms, what do Maine and Europe have in common? Answer: Cape Elizabeth.

According to David L. Kendall's *Glaciers & Granite*, the warped rock of the Cape was once part of the pre-European continent. This was before it was warped. One understands that a move of such magnitude (splitting continents) could only be accomplished by forces great enough to twist rock—force, heat, pressure enough to buckle the ponderous plates of oceanic floors and shove continents willy-nilly. More recent changes include the bending and denuding of the entire lower third of the state by those crystalline giants, the glaciers. Maine has only just rebounded from that colossal event. Great changes these, but with time frame to match: 500 million and one million years respectively. Leaving volcanism aside, it takes nature almost forever to change large expanses of rock. Rocks can be altered by minute forces in stages, as with incremental dismantling process of lichens, water solutions, frost-wedging. Thousands of years are tied up in these mechanisms, yet they are quick-change compared to the slow subduction of lithospheric plates or the tireless prodigious accumulation of glaciers—flake upon flake.

But the air is an element of an altogether different character from those forces beneath our feet. The atmosphere above our heads is ephemeral and swift in comparison. Semantically it's best not confined to that space above our heads, for it encircles and infiltrates our own bodies continuously. Momently we fill our lungs, and even the cells of our flesh respire. We commingle among gases, constantly exchanging gas for gas in this friendly reciprocal atmosphere.

Or is it so friendly? We know that it is not as kind as before. We know that it has begun to change, that progress is rapidly altering it—perhaps beyond our powers of repair. The great surging jet stream, the forceful fronts, milky swirling low-pressure systems, the spacious aerial mountains of airborne particles, all within the generous water cycle by which everything is washed—all these thunderous atmospheric mechanisms are changing. And, according to Senator George Mitchell's *World on Fire*, when the oceans have sopped up as much CO_2 as they can hold in solution, our atmosphere will become that of a hothouse. The projection, made by Goodwin Obasi, secretary-general of the World Meteorological Organization, is for 50 to 100 years. A mere flake on the surface of geologic time. But they don't yet know how these effects will play out.

As I entered the bruised and blasted neighborhood of my backyard my breathing was labored. The atmosphere, as in recent days, was heavy with low-level ozone, and my skin sticky with excess humidity, as though the heaviness of the hothouse were already upon me. About my feet the weathered ruins of our air cleaners lay everywhere, crumpled and broken, going only to decay and the eventual blessedness of soil. Leaves, curled and brown, crackled to dust beneath my tread. I stepped gingerly and high where broken branches of a once respiring life lay in heaps and tangles. Yet many trees still stood. This was no clearcut, but a better kind. Selective cutting. But scraggly standing bits of life, spindly and tall, were themselves bruised and torn by the skidder and many would not fully recover from their wounds, bearing hence the slow-wrecker of insectan pests and disease.

Down I came, picking my way over a river of bones, fascinating leavings broken, stripped bare. Some were pummeled to shreds. The skulls of granite, formerly hidden in soil and leaves, now popped into view. I teetered on twisted bones of boughs across stagnant pools on which swirled the resin of trees. Stumps were coated pale blue with caked sap, the dried outpourings of their vascular systems. The sweet odor of cut wood lingered, diminished and stale. The loggers, tough daring workers who support our woods economy and who must make a living for their families, had moved on to other forests weeks ago.

I clambered down, passing without seeing the flash of white revealing our neighbor's house: I just kept walking, fascinated, upon the undulant river of bones. Then I awoke seeing the pale solid wall through skimpy trees: the lot of the wood-turning mill whose owners, in providing work for our community, had taken wood away.

Enthralled, I had gone too far, missing the path back to my house.

Comment: In its atmospheric changes, Maine will change. It will become a warm place to live but a dangerous place in which to raise kids in the sun. We will have ozone we don't need at depths where we do our breathing, and at heights where we need it for protection from ultraviolet rays we won't have it. *Nemo me impune laccessit.* This may be the future of Maine.

I'd rather fall into a thicket of thistles.

CQ from Maine

WHEN ALLEN WAS UNEMPLOYED last summer, he hankered for a shortwave radio. It would engage his mind and fill his time while he looked for work. From salvage on his previous job he had some old radio tubes and was able to trade them for a vacuum tube Halicrafters receiver in mint condition. He set it under the eaves on a low table, made from a shutter someone had given us, across from my desk. Night after night I heard the strange squealings and squawkings, the rapid *da dits*; voices and languages invisibly thronging the air from over the vast worldscape. Otherwise, in the starry night out my window, I had thought the mighty culture of human beings asleep in the dark.

He borrowed some code cassettes and began practicing American Morse code in earnest. I too began: playing, rewinding and playing the tape machine, practicing to discern electric emanations of dots and dashes and what was signified by them. At first being confident of learning to receive and ultimately send the weird signals, I found that despite the body of discipline connected with writing I've little discipline in things less engaging to me. After two weeks I begrudged the time and dropped the pursuit. What little I learned soon fell through cracks in the neurons—gone.

But Allen is a different sort. He could determine what was encoded, transmitted, but had little hope of using the code to communicate on air: His radio was a receiver, not a transceiver—something he couldn't afford. Yet, he learned and then relearned it all over again a year later when he was finally able to pursue the interest. Today he possesses more than code and license, that token of sanction from the FCC. Today he has a seven-year-old 1983 electronic Kenwood TS-830S, a good used transceiver. He has begun to transmit both signals and voice.

But first he had to string his antenna.

Allen stopped at the local sporting goods store for an arrow, some bowstring and fishing line. He needed these things to hunt and gather signals out of the air. In the backyard is a white pine so high he cannot see the top of it while standing in the yard. Sunshine lights the trunk's tall girthy sides with long patches of white. It is massive and bright, surrounded by boughs clean into heaven.

(Very still is this treeful of life. Sometimes, when looking up into it, one gets that feeling: you may never again be able to claim you were ignorant of things hallowed.)

The bow is bent and strung. The arrow's shaft is wrapped in identifying red tape—in case it lands in the woods among foliage. He takes a spool fishing line and attaches an end of it to the arrow. Upward is the path to the ionosphere where Allen will find his quarry.

(Or, are you casting your weighted line into deep heaven? The signal is every bit of invisible. All you have is rumors of the *direction* in which to point your copper wire.)

His feet in work boots are planted, his grip firm on the bow. The feathered shaft is taut in the bowstring, and drawn.

(You tilt your head, face the sky—hard clear blue. Maybe you feel the gaze of your wife, who stands by. She's taking mental notes on the way you look with your curved bow: arrow pointed, fierce and ardent toward the sky.)

Nothing is now more engaging than this. He aims for the boughs, he lets fly.

The red-wrapped arrow goes. With a treetop so immense and remote, the arrow is in the sky. It arcs over a furry lower branch. It falls, bouncing lightly off a few boughs, to the ground.

(You had thought it would miss, go wildly through the heights and disappear in woods beyond. Instead, it lands in the yard a few feet away.)

He moves to gather the fishing line doubled over the bough, hanging down and blown in a slight breeze. The branch is firmly hooked. He attaches the copper wire to this line and pulls it into air. He walks down to the massive trunk of the pine and secures the fishing line to it with an eyebolt. The wire is now pointed toward invisible and unfamiliar stars, light years beyond the hard bright blue above us. All he needs is to attach the shining copper to a cable sticking from the house. It will route the quarry to his transceiver on its way to ground.

CQ from Maine

(You'll be ready to get on the air, to climb upon signals or send out your voice.)

Allen came bounding downstairs into the kitchen, laughing. "I'm embarrassed. I was calling CQ on 'phone. When I said the last two call letters... it came out sounding *X-way Qwabec*. Like Elmer Fudd would say it."

Autumn approaches. It's time for Allen to sit at the radio, hunkering down for a season before its glowing dials. Wichita Falls, Texas is calling CQ. CQ: the term used to call for a response. Our son, JD, says, "Sounds like 'seek you' to me."

A strumming of crickets pulses outside the night window. WB5 whiskey foxtrot Juliet has a signal of five nine, on a mere twelve watts. Excellent reception: the nine for strength and five for readability.

Fremont, California; station KG6KC is driving around in daylight with a mobile unit in his car. He sends Allen voice signal out a 4-foot whip antenna—in one skip off the ionosphere.

"This one's a copper wire strung into a pine tree," returns Allen.

KG6KC is working as many stations as he can, saying, "73s," and moving on. We hear him next on 'phone to Australia; his four-foot whip and our pine tree wire are now receiving a voice emanating from under the vast turning world.

The next night. After three hours on 'phone, Allen works the ten meter band in code. His blond head is clamped between headphones where he sits under the eaves, fingers pulsing on the key. Laughter erupts from him.

"What?" I call it from my place on the bed, book in hand.

He turns, removing the headphones. "I was trying to call CQ from Maine. It came out 'CQ from Man.'"

Hurricane Tree

THE WORLD IS WASHED with yesterday's rain. I want to go out and eat some of it, to pick what remains of ripe blackberries—the season is passing, past. The time to pick apples is *now*. The finishing of foliage is in Creation's hand. (It is dark, chewed, ragged, changing hue.) Everything is heavy with beads of silver. I touch a young aspen, and it rains on me several moments. Then the return from roadside ravaged thickets to eat blackberries and cereal. I sit now at this oaken table to write about picking apples.

Last month we had a hurricane to finish off the semi-drought. I read that damage by wind to Southern Maine apple trees was severe. According to the *Sun-Journal*, orchard trees were blown down. Uprooted. Apples pummeled each other and the ground, crushing the tender pome inside its skin. Such crushing ruins fruits but makes for good cider. Atomize the pulp, advises one 19th-century cider maker.

Apple Ridge is where I went to pick apples, south and east of home. I'd never seen the place before, never driven those beautiful roads. It was exciting, refreshing . . . oh, those new old roads. They fell in lines beneath mackerel-and-blue sky; I passed fallow fields full of stiff asters and goldenrod waist deep.

Driving down long ridges on my way to the orchard I recalled the storm, Hurricane Bob, having ravaged our east coast on the day of an attempted coup in the decomposing Soviet Union. The news services were full of photos of Boris Yeltsin atop a tank, defying conspirators. The Soviet storm put the finish to the Union of Eastern Europe, signaling widespread disintegration, owing to ethnic strife. The concerted repression of the Communist era was broken, perhaps freeing a welter of pent strife between groups with ancient grievances. One can only wait to find what the ripple effect of the storm will be, worldwide. Will it mean political paralysis and convulsions? Or signal peace and relief from nuclear apprehension? Who

Hurricane Tree

now can know? By the time this is published—in the 21st century—we may know something.

The fruit trees came into view, crammed end-to-end with graceful boughs in colors like fading roses. Visible from the road, the orchard seemed hardly harmed by the hurricane—reportedly one thousand trees had been blown over. I could see some were propped with posts although still thick with fruit. There's probably no better emblem of grace than a branch pointing skyward, encrusted with leaves and globes of fruit. Still, among many thousands of trees, this particular orchard's loss in yield owing to Hurricane Bob was reportedly twenty to twenty-five percent. I had been thinking yet of the trounced and radiating thistle bush we saw in Portland. The storm, I mused, had dropped a bucket-load, felling the bush directly.

Pull up on grass beside the canopy where a scale is set. The attendant points out a road designated for that day's pick-your-own harvest. I get out my doubled paper bag and walk back within the privacy of fruit trees in flanking walls. Boles are thick and squat, crusty with gray flaking bark. Branching begins waist high but, diverted by childish memories and historical research, I clamber awkwardly into the branching web of one, then laugh at my ridiculous position: These are not those high trees of history, of my childhood—great sky-bound things. Limbs are low enough here to pick while standing on the ground. The apples, all Macintosh, are large and rosy and greenish. Green on one side, rosy on the other, delicately coated with bloom. I am amazed at the speed with which the shopping bag fills.

It was filled, then I saw the prone hurricane tree. I saw it first from behind, and thought it just a very low tree branching fully in canopy and crown.... Walking around... seeing it lying on the ground and thick with apples... tangled in vines of bright red berries. Using *Newcomb's Wildflower Guide*, which has blossoms for clues, it's hard to identify a plant that has gone into fruit... but indications are that the vine was bittersweet nightshade. The cupping calyx at the base of the fruit was a five-pointed star. I happened to step on some of these berries as I walked around the tree and noticed that they were like thin-skinned tiny seedy tomatoes. Even their runny pome was markedly similar.

Mrs. Grieve says the name derives from the dual taste of root and stem, which, when chewed, tastes bitter then sweet. Solanine, contained within (and accounting for the bitterness), will paralyze the central nervous system. She lists agonizing symptoms, including convulsions ending in death.

Visiting the Eastern Uplands

I walked around the prone tree and saw that much of its root system was still buried, but an upper portion clung loosely and ineffectually to the soil. The base was wrapped in chicken wire and there were two fallen props, one supine, one tilted, still clinging to the crux of branches spread like stiff arms. Enmeshed and tangled in vines of bittersweet nightshade, with its dangling clusters of poisonous vivid berries, the hurricane tree was a heartbreakingly fair sight. Looking around, I noticed not another like it.

Plucking away, I topped off my brown bag from its fallen crown. One last glance, a tug to loosen a specimen of the vine for later identification, and I walked back down between fruited walls toward the road.

On the drive to Rumford, where I was due to pick up Allen, I took valley roads never taken before. One clove straight through Turner which, according to the Lewiston *Sunday*, earns more of the Maine farming dollar than any other town in the state. News to me: I'd thought Aroostook—The County—would yield the highest producing town. As a bedroom community, the population here has doubled in the last fifteen years, but amazingly the land in agriculture has also gained. According to the Good Shepherd Food-Bank newsletter, *More Than Food*, a goodly amount of its greens and yellows—peppers cucumber zucchini eggplants carrots summer squash beans and apples—find their way into the stomachs, cells and bones of people with little to spend on that most vital of riches: food. For example, Benjamin Taylor Pre-pak produce handlers have donated just such vegetables to the Food-Bank.

This new-to-me road was heavy with foliaged and flowered old houses, as though a straight branch encrusted with leaves and globes of fruit. I daydream along the road here looking at them . . . even about publishing a book of my own some day; deciding that if I ever get an inheritance, I will. In the 21st century event, Allen offered and paid to publish it for me. *Return to God's House*, by name. This is grace, I thought. Bound from the sky. These are the many mansions.

Father Word

WHAT IS IT ABOUT that word? *Aroostook.* "The County," they call it in Maine.

A word is a tiny thing, a written word. It is smaller than a leaf—a word printed on a page. Rarely as big as a blade of grass. Don't even bother comparing its size to a tree. And yet.... Words conjure trees: trees doubled by wind ... a hemlock, its crown pushed down, boughs thrashing on a gale.

A word is a little member, but mighty. You lay one behind another, but they bunch up and pile themselves into structures, images, emoting pictures. They breathe on you, rousing. An idea is extended, whole houses of mentalities.... Flowers are identified by them, the contents of fields. Plots are sold, injustices revealed, societies laid bare. Little word.

Stone. Or, fish. Arrow. Branch.

Heart/core. They resonate. All primal, designating. We sit and turn pagefuls. We work for years placing a bookful, just so. Each and every word. They are read in hours, forgotten in moments ... or change the course of lives.

What mystery is housed in the word *forest*? Evergreen boughs upturned in mist, crowned with cones. And breathing leaves. Respiring vapors, fragrance. Exchanging gases with humans who shelter beneath.

Words are but symbols for associations. Fine lines (minute fragments) are curved, spliced, intersected with precision, black on white ... only to invoke something, not themselves. A written word knows it is nothing, hides itself to give you ... a *fish*—iridescent with gills, twitching there in the shallows.

Fish and Stone, and Arrow and Tree are all Anglo-Saxon in origin. They are primal, mythopoeic. This is what J.R.R. Tolkien said, mythologist and master of words. A mighty philologist, he was called by words. According to T.A. Shippey in his book, *Road to Middle-earth*, the language

Visiting the Eastern Uplands

of Goths (Gothic) fueled Tolkien's passion—although its fragments were few. The language could only be inferred, so little was known of it. Scraps preserved in script, that's all.

One scrap is *atta Attila*, or daddy Attila, a reference to Attila the Hun. Tolkien relished it. Hearing these words stirred the word-master, because they imparted volumes of understanding about the Goths, who were overrun and their heritage plundered by Huns. So why was Attila, who was their destroyer, referred to by them with familial devotion? This phrase salted the spectacle of legend, of antiquity, for Tolkien, demonstrating that Goths joined their enemies in spoiling their own heritage. And I find it is salient metaphor of humanity's spiritual heritage: a fall from Paradise, telling ourselves a story, forsaking the truth.

Try the word *Story* itself. From the *American Heritage Dictionary*: via Middle English, Norman French, Latin (*historia*), Greek: Wisdom. In story we have the source and house of our imaginations. Marriage and divorce are each results of stories we tell ourselves. Heads—of both the grossest criminal and the most thoughtful astrophysicist—teem with theories, stories phrased in numbers, words. (Numbers are also words.)

Now try *county*. The County.

Aroostook.

I sat in the Ohio kitchen with books spread out, having just read a word. I said the word aloud. Someone little called. A door whanged. I stood automatically, walked three steps, reached up and got out peanut butter. There was white cold milk in the refrigerator, and soft bread speckled with cracked wheat on the counter. The word *Aroostook* was thickening against the roof of my mouth.

It's been years, but that's how I remember it. I'd like to go there. However, driving the Town Road today, my spouse Allen asks, "Why Aroostook? Why is it so important to you?"

The word must be highly selective.

It was the back road, going toward our own county seat. The Western Maine ponds—limpid, green, and cut with lights—were behind us in a fold of the old hills.

My words now were purely explanatory: about that Ohio kitchen twelve years behind. About the endless prehistoric forest in some corner of a distant northern state. About that forest's ablation into a sea of pine stumps; each five, six, or seven feet in diameter. And of how potatoes now grew in their stead. Aroostook was now an aisle of civilization bordering a rolling plain of farms, edging, in turn, a great industrial north woods filled with thin trees. And I had been listening to its story.

Aroostook, I said, is the mystique of exploring Aroostook.

What I did not say was that I explore words, search out their sounds, meanings and mysteries. Use them to evoke more mystery. I write words because I am called by the Word.

Going North beneath the Moon

It is a road and night to suit the mystery. We've been traveling northward velvet miles, mile upon mile unfurling, the feel of newly poured asphalt below, an endless whirring of the Subaru's engine, the occasional dip and rise of road beneath its tires. Ahead we follow anonymous red winking gems, just disappearing around some shadowy curve filled with black shapes of trees. Eastward floats a scalloped sheen of clouds, turning silver as a moon rises among them. In the west, a crack of pale light splits the dark from end-to-end along our horizon. The sun has gone below the fringed fastness of Maine; seemingly all its forested Aroostook north-west-land lying deserted and dark.

Now comes a pointy-eared coyote loping toward us beneath the berm of the roadway, faintly golden in our high-beams. The animal disappears behind.

We are hushed, back to watching the sky above the celestial roadway. We peel along this stretch as through marbled night, wakefulness cast over our minds. On and on we rush down this shimmering dark, on and on as the dark deepens.

The sky is changing before our eyes, but so steadily that we do not recognize a moment of transition despite our watchfulness. Where minutes before a scalloped sheen of clouds covered a darkened sky, now the scallops themselves darken, and sky behind them turns bright. For darkness has just changed places with the light.

Hidden from direct view, the moon ascends. If a chorus has been singing a quiet hymn of holiness over our heads, its song now sinks to a humming. Humming of darkness and light.

The root word for vegetable in Latin means lively or full of life. The same would apply to the word vegetate, from which we derive vegging-out—something we might do before the TV night after night. Opposites are contained in the word.

They razzed Allen where he works in the mill. They called him "Spuds." Why let your wife drag you way up there, hundreds of miles to—to potato fields? Nothing up there but tubers. Some broccoli. Industrial woodlands. Why drive six hours to vegetables?

It's an old question: "Why all this fuss about Aroostook?" It's a quote more than 120 years old, made by a Boston newspaper man in the late 1800s, at an exhibition in the Bay City. Farmers up here needed an extended railroad linking their bountiful land to markets of the East Coast, the nation, the world. They went to Boston in order to showcase their produce, wares and wood products . . . to that vast moneyed population which could surely use these. Yet there were few takers. According to Clarence A. Day, in his *Farming in Maine, 1869 to 1940*, the Northern Maine Railroad Company was started in 1887 but soon failed. For the perception was as the newspaper man had declared: "There's nothing up there but bears and Indians."

And spuds.

Why this persisting perverse tone?

Even people in Maine today . . . who are willing to work sometime 16 hours a day in vast blooming concrete caverns where the sun does not shine . . . where paper is made of substance no longer recognizable as vegetable . . . where respirators are required in case of hydrogen sulfide or chlorine dioxide leaks. . . . If it weren't for fishing and hunting they'd be in danger of forgetting vegetation and fresh air.

The perception has seeped south of Boston today. The Congress in Washington DC ruled that Loring Air Force Base in Limestone, near the Canadian border in The County, would be phased out precisely because of this negative point of view. These lawmakers, who work in offices where pressed and chemically pulped vegetables are shuffled, seem happier without potatoes growing under their windows. The Defense Base Closure and Realignment Commission voted to close the base—in direct opposition to law, which specified that closing criteria relate to our nation's defense: they voted to close because the Air Force did not care for Aroostook's "quality of life."

Spuds.

Visiting the Eastern Uplands

But the darkness of our moral landscape has swapped places with the light . . . over the protracted course of our industrialization (and cyberization), and we are all in danger of forgetting vegetables and fresh air. We want to be on the Celestial Highway, progressive. We want lifts to take us out of The Valley of Humiliation so we can ski the Delectable Mountains. We desire to pass over the Slough of Despond without stopping to learn how to fish.

In the singing darkness Allen and I cross over an imaginary line. Our earthly position becomes The County, Aroostook. The eastern upland country of Maine. The surrounding dark land will be pricked with tiny white lights as exits for Island Falls, Oakfield, Smyrna Mills pass.

Then we see it: the sign for Houlton, and the terminus of I-95, end of the interstate in the USA. Nothing but pinpricks of white upon a distant curve, lying northeast in blackness beneath the moon.

Breakfast at the Elm Tree

BEFORE RETIRING TO BED at the American Motel on Route 2a, I stepped out for a pint of milk and a newspaper at a funky neighborhood store in the gateway town of Houlton.

"What does Aroostook mean?" I asked the congenial counterman. His smile was a bit sheepish, as he said he didn't know. Maybe I should have stopped asking there, but instead I asked, "How'd Mars Hill up the road get that name?" Again he shook his head, but then he brightened, saying he just learned that his hometown of Patten was named for an early settler.

Settlers' names, Indian place names, foreign cities and countries, compass points, coastal geographic features, biblical places, all largely comprise the names of Maine's villages and towns. Houlton, I knew from reading Clarence Day, was named for Joseph Houlton, a pioneer of the New Salem Academy Grant.

At that time in 1805 there was no railroad. There was no road, period, connecting his homestead with the rest of Maine. And Houlton, if I remember right, was the first Yankee to grow potatoes in Aroostook. (The French to the north had been at it in prior decades.)

In the dark last night we missed the white sign with black letters posted beside the highway, an historical marker. We saw it this morning on our way to the Elm Tree Diner on the Old Bangor Road just south of Houlton. Now, sitting in a booth, our orders taken, I jot down a note about it: *Military Road, built 1828*. I remember reading about this first road in Day's book. There was going to be a struggle with Great Britain over an imaginary line: the borderline of two vast countries filled with big timber. The conflict called for a road through dense, canopied woodland; through trees towering and thick enough to blot out the sky. The road outside his door was cut as far as this place on the current Canadian border, as far as this

Visiting the Eastern Uplands

southern-most settlement . . . with all of Aroostook, roadless, stretching away into the vast darkness of the North.

Breakfast at the Elm Tree Diner, home cooking since 1945. "Your home away from home," according to the postcard which features the long white contours of the diner. The smell of bacon, biscuits and coffee. It's busy, crammed with people, but I plan to stoke up a bit of conversation with our waitperson. She appears to be about 17 years old, dressed in crisp powder blue, wearing a happy ponytail. At first glance she might be thought perky. One would think her bubbly and pitying. One would be wrong. She is as hard-boiled and entrenched as any social worker in any of our hard-boiled, entrenched cities.

Aroostook, she says, is an Indian word whose meaning eludes her. She leaves us coffee and continues her rounds. The place is hopping but she is unruffled, efficient in the performance of her duties. Businesslike and ready at half my age. . . . I would be harassed under performance pressures like these.

Allen likes this diner, he likes its name. It's an Elm Tree morning. He talks about the tree, elegiac, for he remembers it from childhood. He had them in his yard growing up but can't recall much except that they died of Dutch elm disease, leaving nothing but a memory of the contour of leaves. Death by blight. For my part, I remember only the disease . . . hearing of it . . . the regretful talk of my elders. That the adjacent boulevard was lightened by their departure. Yellowing foliage followed by defoliation and slow death (so say the books), caused by fungus carried by bark beetles.

"There are plenty of elms in Maine now," I tell him. "I see them when we drive around." And it is the contour of the entire tree I recall, not the leaf. I've never been able to reach a leaf to examine its outline.

The young waitperson returns with our meal. I ask her about the ambitions of Houlton's youth. What will they do for a living? She answers by telling me a bit about herself. She is a senior at the University of Maine, studying sociology, and planning to return to Houlton as a social worker. She commutes home on weekends to work this job. Ambitious herself, her assessment of local ambitions is, however, stereotypical. That is, children of the college-educated go to college, while children of laborers become laborers: the latter will work in farming and logging until they "come to other alternatives." What these are she does not say. She leaves for another order and I dutifully jot down these considered observations. As though a social worker.

We drive around Houlton, chuckling over the cassette recorder, and enter the Market Square Historic District. Are cinemas historic? Yes, but not in this ambient context. The streets are lined with younger trees under pre-turn of the-20th-century brick blocks. Many tall three-story blocks with rows of arched windows lining top floors. The French Block, for one, 1894. Shops on the ground floor: Towne & Country Clothing, Bangor Savings, Damascus Inspirational Gifts, JCPenney, Ernie's Comic Books (used books, old magazines, collectibles). The buildings give an impression of being a few stories higher than they are. Ceilings were high and decorous in those more spacious days. We leave downtown and drive to an area of graciously shaded old homes. We're looking for elm trees.

"See that knob of tree in the distance—projecting over the others?" The elm has a rounded top with fountained branches, stately and tall. We head for it.

The gingerbread house itself is quite old, white, in need of scraping and painting. It has piazzas, a portico, rusty wrought-iron gates, and raptors surmounting gateposts at the drive entrance. The elm is exceedingly high and shapely, towering over the old mansion.

This is Houlton, the first incorporated Aroostook town. Will we dine beneath elm trees? Tonight we will dine in The County.

Aroostook County, Ohio

LEAVING HOULTON. WE PASS a potato truck admirably heaped with great potatoes. The truck is circa 1940s, but painted purple and green, with patched fenders, in the distinctive potato-truck shape, still contemporary: Its bed is like a giant trough, its sides hinged boards girt in steel.

Traveling north on Route 1, en route for Presque Isle. Scanning out the window I note a whole lot more sky up here than we are used to in the Western Mountains. I'm struck. Instantly reminded of Ohio's sky-vastness, counterpane in shades of gray. This landscape looks like Ohio with its rolling hills and white farms, interstitial wood lots, and lines of trees. I could think of this as the Ohio of Maine, the countrified Midwest of the North. It's been said that the eventual opening of Aroostook by rail inoculated many would-be emigrants against the so-called Ohio Fever spreading throughout rock-bound Maine in the mid and late 1900s. Instead of leaving Maine, these folks came here to farm. Nevertheless the famous fever effectively drained this state of its youth and verve, but not all who succumbed fled to Ohio. Many new states and territories in the West and Midwest were beneficiaries of Maine's acumen and Yankee perseverance. The drain put a cap on our state's population growth so severe it would be another hundred years before its population broke one million.

We're passing a vivid green farm yard dotted with bright orange pumpkins. We pass another displaying shiny shields of used hubcaps. I reach into the backseat to grab an apple. It's a large one, picked from the hurricane tree in Western Maine, still with the bloom on it. My teeth slash through the tough green-rosy skin and my lips pucker with its swift tartness. My mouth full, I make crunching noises as I report on the landscape into the tape recorder.

Here, where we travel our route of exploration, streams have a different orientation from all others in the state. They flow northward, draining only by circuitous route and through another country into the Gulf of Maine. They cut through rich loamy soils like those of the Midwest and drain rolling ridges of glacial till covered with fields and crops.

In *Glaciers & Granite,* David L. Kendall writes that the soils, called Caribou loams, derive from limestone bedrock that was crushed by the continental glacier. Evidence is cited in *The County: Land of Promise,* edited by Anna Fields McGarth, saying that Aroostook may have had its own mini glacier: the rocks left behind to crop up in farmers' potato fields are The County's own—small and brown like the potatoes themselves—scarcely like the monstrous granitic erratics found in southern, western and central mountainous regions of the state.

We're still marveling over this great expanse of lumpy sky, as we search the horizon for an anomaly—that's what Allen calls it at first sight: Mars Hill is shaped like a volcano, jutting above rolling land in the north. Dark, protruding above this vast horizon, it looks classical, godly. Although it's made of sedimentary rock—causing one to think glaciers would've disposed of it with ease—Mars Hill is weather-resistant conglomerate and sandstone; conglomerate being a compacted jumble of rocks cemented together by plutonic pressures, weight of the mountainous earth pressing upon itself. Weight enough to form solid metamorphic rock of sedimentary rock and sediments.

Cresting one of the long Ohio-like ridges, we look off eastward toward the blue undulate Canadian horizon. Now we pass through an intersection with sign pointing east to New Brunswick and the border crossing. Florence and Centerville: English names those, not the French we had expected. Again we top some roll of land and Mars Hill startles us, rearing into view. It enlarges, spreading a good presence above ripe farmland.

New homes are rare, if present at all on this stretch. So many are old and tilting, sagging. There are also large solid farmhouses, white and old-fashioned. Allen says this appearance seems little changed in a hundred years. The old-style potato barns are in various stages of decline. The weight of snow borne over decades has made them sway-back. These gambrel-roofed barns are no longer built for use in the industry, though we will find evidence—in newer dwellings farther north—of a continuing fondness for the design. Gambrel roofs, topping basement foundations, protrude above surrounding properties, like godly Mars Hill above eastern Aroostook.

We're rounding the mountain itself, and slowly it lengthens. Its western side is revealed a great ridge, as though a body of earth-tree-rock, lying on its side, streaked green with ski trails. Houses line the road below: The village of Mars Hill with its low buildings apparently lying across our course. Potato trucks drive through with their heavy heaped loads, the harvest. A sign says, Presque Isle, only fourteen miles north, and Caribou but thirteen beyond that.

Outside the village we pass a big aluminum building with stacks of large wooden crates: manufacturer of potato bins? Broccoli bins? According to a helpful booklet put out by the UM Cooperative Extension Service, *Growing Potatoes in Maine*, 90% of the state's crop is shipped during the cold months. Storage bins are small, 12 x 20, or as large as 18 x 30—the tubers being piled eighteen feet deep inside.

We speed on through the heartland. Mars Hill, its backside long and low, and having lost its volcanic shapeliness, slides back. The foliage here is deep crimson, splashing orange, and flaming red. A self-service potato stand pops up. A field of dried brown potato plants, vine-killed, awaits harvest. Such top-killing prevents the spread of blight from plant to tuber. This also toughens potato skins, lessening the possibility of bruising. And it's easier to harvest top-killed potatoes.

The tree farm, neat pine nursery, stripes a hillside as we pass. Quaggy Joe Mountain arises. But harvesting has my attention and, passing a neat row of white trailers, we pull off the road. An earthen field beckons. I look out to see small tan-colored piles of what looked like potatoes. In days not long past, potatoes were unearthed by mechanical "diggers". They lay spotting the surface of soil until picked by the hands of children. Today picking is done with mechanical "harvesters," a more complex machine. But these piles beside the car are *not* potatoes, but angular sedimentary rocks the size and color of potatoes.

I climb from the car into a brisk cool wind. We're on a ridge amid many undulated potato fields in various stages of harvest. Some are still dark leafy green and have yet to be top-killed. Some are weathered, awaiting harvest. And some are rich and loamy, full of turned Ohio-like soil and empty of potatoes, stripped of food.

I step onto the edge of this earthy field. A few potatoes lie here and there. Some have been smashed by the mechanical harvester, but others are still good and could be gleaned. I stoop to steal a couple. They are buff-colored, dimpled with textured skin, rough beneath my thumb. Standing here with the Aroostook wind blowing across me, across the fields, I'm shivering. My feet kick absently at shredded leavings of pulped vines reminding me of the smashed-to-ribbon bits of trees found in skidder yards beside the woods.

I look out into the wind toward the spread patchwork of fields. The fields surrounding are dug up, brown but crisscrossed with green—the boundaries of other fields defined in trees. There in the distance is a tiny grouping of harvester and truck, appearing motionless, going about the ponderous mechanical business of gathering tubers. There, high-schoolers (perhaps) stand on the rumbling platform, slinging rotten spuds and rocks from conveyors. It's all too small for me to see distinctly. I don't see the people: I see machines.

I breathe in on a sigh. Being in The County, where clipped farmland presents so spread a sky, is like seeing from the top of a mountain. It is symbolically appropriate that one finds Aroostook at the top of the Maine map. But, if you are at this moment in an Ohio farmhouse and want to see the view from a mountaintop, go out the back door, step well away from the house, and turn a 360.

You're now on top of the world, looking out from the heavenly perspective on a realm full of food or the powerful potential for food.

Yet there *is* some difference between Ohio and The County: When I climb at last into the warm and buttoned up Subaru with Allen, I'm greeted with melodious French, the voice of a young woman flowing from the radio.

Monuments

WE TAKE TO THE highway again and now the long wooded ridge of Green and Quaggy Joe Mountains flanks our route. This is the true volcanic relic mentioned in books. Its composition is rhyolite, according to *Glaciers & Granite*, fine-grained rock, volcanic, composed like granite. It is part of the rim of an ancient caldera (a vast volcanic basin). These descriptions mean that this ridge was formed in a process whereby great balloons of hot lava ascended through the plastic mantle of earth, in much the same manner as that of Maine's Western Mountains. But unlike them, these balloons of molten rock pushed clean through the overlying sedimentary rock to cool upon the smoking surface: each a naked monument to its own plutonic power. This happened in a geologic epoch when continents were colliding, and hell raised up an explosive head to cast its flaming looks around. The resulting rhyolite monument lacks the crystallinity of the western plutons—which, molten, cooled beneath crustal surfaces.

There's a sign: *Aroostook State Park*. We turn, follow. The park contains Quaggy Joe. Looking along its massive double-peaked length, hunkered beneath this bounded sky and perforce blocking the western view, we realize afresh that climbing mountains gets them out of the way. So that they no longer block the view.

We round a corner below the northerly peak of Quaggy Joe. There's another road sign—about a trans-Atlantic flight monument. How incongruous. What's *that* doing in farm country, potato land?

But, moving toward it, our attention is caught by surprisingly graceful expressions of old age: one of those weathered gambrel-roofed potato barns in mid-collapse. Its old roof has almost caved in. The upright dark-windowed farmhouse opposite (with paint worn off) is fronted by old-fashioned bushes, tall spindly yellow flowers. A large dead elm (with bark gone) stands starkly in the yard, claimed by blight. Two more lie near, as naked,

Monuments

and one of these is being sawn asunder by an old man with a saw. Henry Beetle Hough, a crusty New England newspaper man and himself an old man at the time, wrote in 1976 about the Dutch elm fungal attack. It wasn't a natural occurrence, but resulted from an advance of transportation, communication in this ravenous age. The blight is called Dutch elm disease because the fungus shipped over from Europe. Also in this transportation metaphor: roots meeting underground in a neighborhood tended to pass the fungus around. Transport is a powerful analogy full of implications for all levels of human interaction. Yet, in comparison with these giant plants, consider how slight that filamentous body of attacking fungi that ultimately destroys the tree.

Here, in these emblems of house and elm and barn, find slow physical ruin viewed on a somber day by two excited mid-lifers on an exploratory journey. This scene is the old age of Aroostook, breeding such grace as to make one almost desire such a lingering passage. I cannot view it without elegy. Someone, Somewhere, finds it precious, grave and true.

We are approaching the monumental launch site of the first successful trans-Atlantic balloon flight—? Never heard of it.

What are we looking at? There, at the end of a walk lined with autumnal marigolds, stands a tall black-and-silver replica of a helium balloon. The whole plot is enclosed in freshly stained rail fence. Imagine the fame of this site, had the feat been performed 100 years ago. It would rival Kitty Hawk and be in history books. But I have never heard of the historic flight before.

Allen says maybe they are hurting for monuments in this part of the country. He hurries away from me up the walk toward this replica.

I stop outside the fence to inspect a marker set in conglomerate rock. Crisp, colorful chunks of rock have been compacted together by the weight of earth. Speckled rock—white bluish brown buff gray, even pink. A plaque designates this monument: the *Maxi Anderson Memorial Park,* 1935–1983. Who the heck is Maxi Anderson?

The gravel walk beckons, benches set on either side. The two-toned balloon replica looms large as I approach, a silver bulbous top tapering down to a black narrow cone. Allen brushes past on his way back to the car. He seems to have gained a bit of respect, murmuring that I not miss the foot marker.

Visiting the Eastern Uplands

There are other markers between flanking cedars. One proclaims, "*Launching site of the first successful trans-Atlantic balloon, August* 11–17, *1978; Double Eagle II, Presque Isle, Maine.*"

That recent? Shouldn't that have been a Jules Vernesque feat for the 19th-century? Later in the day I will come across a book by Charles McCarry on the subject and learn that the first attempt, from some other site, was ill-starred. I will see photos of the pilots aloft and a diagram of flight plans. The different ways the wind sent each craft, the short-falling Double Eagle and the successful Double Eagle II. The former took off outside beleaguered Boston and was swept far northward on a course looping and lost, somewhere between Greenland and the north coast of Iceland. The latter craft left a farm field in remote Aroostook to take its eastward course—fair-starred, on target—across to Ireland, Wales and the coast of France. ("Why all this fuss about Aroostook," wrote the 19th-century Boston newspaper man.)

An eleven storey helium balloon, transportation of a less insatiable age, carried the faithful crew through the mighty elements and over Aroostook, New Brunswick, Newfoundland, and the great North Atlantic to land in a grain field in France. Frail in body and craft, wearing oxygen masks, these men were transported to heights of 25,000 ft.; high into the dome of the great cold cathedral, adrift within its vaporous veil. Huddling inside curtains swathing their gondola, they wore arctic clothing. On board were other essentials: pantry and potty, some instruments and logs for navigation and documentation. Gliding soundless in the wind, five miles high and out to sea. In those impossible heights they experienced what few know: no matter how strong the gale, while it bears you away you won't hear of it.

My gaze slips down to the foot of this monument where, between shrubs, a marker is set. The crew are listed, including . . . "*Maxi Anderson, September 10, 1934 to June 27, 1983.*" Someday I will learn of his death-by-practice. It happened on a flight preparatory to circumnavigating earth by balloon. Think of Jules Verne, whose Professor Aronnax spoke to his companions in exhilaration or terror on exiting the Nautilus: "We know how to die."

Yes, this is a monument to people and technology past. To a time before we went beyond the bounds set for safety and humility: a time when we knew our place in earth and how to travel bravely through its elements. In a couple of years, a contest of countries will rise on wind from this field. Balloonists of many nations will strive to cross the Atlantic. Some of these will fall into the sea, and some will have "years taken off their lives" when a sonic boom from the *Concorde* blasts them through those terrible heights. Lines of travel old and new will cross in heaven. In this age Consumerism, with its flaming dependence on fossil fuels, has raised its explosive head to cast insatiable looks around.

But, here below, I stand as the wind buffets this memorial. On either side of this towering replica soar flag-poles bereft of flags. Empty lines knocking, knocking in the wind.

We travel a back road toward the highway, leaving the trans-Atlantic monument behind. From below we can look up toward US Route 1. There, on the ridge where it runs, stand three distant elm trees, tiny, high as heaven, remote. In foliage just beginning to turn.

Touring Presque Isle

I'M THINKING OF CHRISALLER'S patterns of population distribution. Here in Aroostook I think of those patterns, whether radiating or linear—lines indicating roads, printed on maps. In Maine's Western Mountains we have the linear pattern. Population centers—towns, villages, hamlets—are strung along a single highway, punctuated at either end by cities, say, Berlin N.H. and Bangor. But here in *The County* one sees a different pattern, one similar to Chrisaller's ideal in which a central place radiates roads to outlying villages and hamlets.

Looking at a map of Ohio, one sees Kenton, west of Marion, smack in the middle of rolling farmland with roads radiating to outlying communities. One sees Hillsboro and Coshocton, centers of similar patterns. I've been to these places, and now, driving around Presque Isle not far from the Canadian border in northeastern Maine, I see the similarity of size and appearance. If Presque Isle's trees were girthy and high, lining its streets—it could be a Wooster, Ohio.

But . . . Presque Isle is "Where the Spirit Still Moves," declares the sign at its entrance. A bold declaration, given the evidence—cited by Rolfe and Mitchell in *Maine: The Geography*—that Aroostook is the only county in Maine to remain unaffected by recent growths in population. And it is looking like there will soon be a drain of current levels: The proposed closure of Loring Air Force Base in nearby Limestone will see to it. Yet, given the mystery of Spirit, I don't dismiss this town's claim.

Allen and I tour Presque Isle, whose name means Almost Island. It might have been a misplaced coral atoll, with its unusual (for Maine) fossils of seabed life. It is different from Houlton, lacking that older town's dark mass of brick blocks. Its buildings are lower, more cheaply constructed, modern tacky-ticky. More of the businesses are familiar to me as chain stores—Ames, Radio Shack, Fashion Bug, IGA; familiar from our part of

Touring Presque Isle

the state. Here's a surprise, a homeless shelter in a church building. Not that the building surprises—it seems appropriate. It is the *need* in this rural setting that jerks one's attention.

Allen wants to see the airport, having read of its role as staging point for the Army Air Corps in World War II. The County is a geographically suited jumping-off point to Europe—for both bombers and balloonists. An appropriate criterion of defense, wouldn't you say? The Airport Park we tour before reaching the airport proper is full of the tinny, tiny and uniform structures one associates with World War II military housing, and also those low Quonset hut warehouses that have been converted to commercial uses. But the airport itself disappoints. There are no leftover B-17 bombers, no signs of a museum.

"What do you expect to find here?" It's hard to believe there was *ever* anything happening here.

"I'm looking for the wheat."

Apparently he's after the kernels left behind from a time when this airport was active. He's thinking of the mighty B-17s and how they shook earth in pursuit of an enemy. His father was one of those pilots. These present decades, with their empty consumer pursuits and culture of convenience, seem far from the bread of that desperate time.

We're driving back toward the center of town, and Allen has spotted a little brown bookshop called . . . *Book Shop*. He pulls up in the Subaru and climbs out, leaving me to blab a few words into the cassette recorder. I've grown fond of this little black spooling machine. Ready to toss my sloppy notebooks and cheap ubiquitous pens. But all this will change when time comes to transcribe. I'll then pay for this seductive ease with tedious marathons of spooling—play and replay. Will be forced to turn engine noises, inarticulate utterings, coughs, guffaws and Allen's scarcely caught phrases into precise ordered experience . . . upon the crisp page.

I glance up at a homemade particleboard sign hanging above the door, painted white and cut in the shape of an open book. Inside the door are stacks and shelves crammed with books, those harbingers of other worlds. I'll go inside to be greeted by the heady evocative *must* of other ages, must of improper storage. *Open on Saturday only.* Must be owned and operated by a teacher?

And, upon entering and easing myself into the conversation-in-progress between Allen and the owner, I find it to be so. She's a helpful, middle-aged California transplant; the strawberry blonde wife of an ex-Air Force

Visiting the Eastern Uplands

man, and herself a fifth-grade teacher. Teachers, we sense in the archetype, hold the keys of knowledge, and trope/token/teacher promptly provides it by telling us about a special key we may yet lay hands upon. This is a key known but to a few, yet available to all.

Get ready.

It is the key to—*The Aroostook Room*. Yes, Virgil, there is an *Aroostook Room*. How the imagination glows—as though someone, seeing a spark, had cupped hands and blown upon it. An archive. A whole roomful of arcana: newspapers, primary documents, maps, books, correspondence. Its location would be a secret worth paying millions for: one should have to pore over a dingy torn map with burned edges, wriggle her way through twenty acres of bog and puckerbrush, fight off a sizable portion of the state's 20,000 bears. But no, says the teacher. The Aroostook Room is simply squirreled away on the second floor of the ummpy library. That's what it sounds like to my culturally-neophyte ear. Being UMPI, the acronym for the University of Maine Presque Isle.

The spacious green campus is adorned with freshly quarried hunks of limestone. We drive a lane lined with bright boulders. A load of fresh stone has been dumped—like unrecognized discarded gold ore—in a cutbank to curb erosion. It's spitting rain but I beg Allen to halt so I can get out and wantonly pluck a souvenir, hefty and hard, from its hoard. Recorder in hand, I breathe a description into it:

" . . . slate-gray colored and kinda marbled, turning yellow in places." The marbling reminds me of gypsum, but is calcite. Glacier-crushed limestone in Aroostook topsoil makes for the production of good loamy soil, hence good crops/food. This crystalline-seeming limestone, compressed of primordial sea life, has quickened my spirit after the long drive. Like an application of gold fever. I'm tipsy over its hardness, beauty and form.

Outside the ummpy library rests a large freshly quarried elegant limestone. Larger than a cubic yard, of irregular shape, it resembles a chunk of faceted solidified clay. Its crown is a rich charcoal-gray slab, marbled with white. The rock's pure mineral beauty surprises me. Looking like giant-sized cake, it almost makes my mouth water. I had thought limestone would be crude, pressed sediment; shelfy, brown and drab. The calcite *will* eventually oxidize to a buff color. Allen estimates that this cuboid elegant precursor to potatoes weighs about 1500 pounds.

Touring Presque Isle

The library turns out to be closed until noon: It's Saturday. Allen wants to drive around and see a little more of Presque Isle while we wait for it to open. I didn't sleep well last night at the American Motel and, as he turns this way and that, find myself drifting off in cramped slumber.

Comes a jolt. I pull the lever to recline. I rouse only when he pulls into the parking lot before a store with a sprawling yellow sign: *VIDEO*. It's the size of a mobile home, that sign. You could read it from space without a satellite telescope. Allen's going to browse its stacks while I stay behind to snooze. He will return wheatless.

TV and its offspring, such miraculous devices. Yet, for all the possibility have they become an assault? And are in their turn assaulted? First, says Donella H. Meadows, adjunct professor of environmental studies at Dartmouth College, where's clarity on how to proceed, since we are loosing the distinction between free speech political, essential in a democracy, and the free speech which is commercial, and undermining. She echoes Edward R. Murrow's warning of 1958: "Unless we get up off our fat surpluses and recognize that television . . . is being used to distract, dilute, amuse and insulate us, then television and those who finance it, those who look at it and those who work at it, may see a totally different picture too late."

I'm ready for a deep doze.

The key is in the ignition, the radio on, set to a French station—must be French-Canadian, not one of Maine's? The male voice is unintelligible to me, tripping and mellow. Restful. I'm almost asleep again. Comes music—rich vibrant sinister passionate. My eyes are closed and I'm a bit numb but no longer sleeping. The voice returns suddenly, interlacing menacing incomprehensible French with sinister music. It blends and rises to riveting crescendo and now I'm stiff with invoked apprehension, ignorant, thrilled. But in the midst of this French, he sneers like a gang-banger in English, repeatedly firing out the words: *"You sure know how to die!"*

The climactic music stops, French ripples out again, flowing, melodious.

A car has pulled up on the driver's side as I lay with eyes closed, far from sleep. Its door creaks open and a man screams: *WAKE UP!* The door slams, the car pulls away.

French ripples innocently from the radio.

A slow smile stretches my lips. You sure know how to make it interesting. Presque Isle.

The Aroostook Room

The Aroostook Room at the University of Maine Presque Isle is not exactly a potato house. A potato house would be cool and concrete, where tubers are packed for storage or shipping—dank and dim and furnished with conveyors for washing and sorting. The potato house provides seasonal jobs, repetitive labor, and a place where warmly dressed workers stand for hours inspecting spuds for shape, size, ripeness, sunburn, scabs and bruises. If you're a purely social being, not lazy, you might have no trouble sinking your teeth into this work.

Other workers, called hangers, stand bagging and handing the bags off to the scaler. Then a worker puts each bag through a tying machine where wire binds the bagtop and sends it onto the next conveyor. Bags are spot-checked for grade by state inspectors. Truck-loading is the end procedure of the potato house. From there potatoes take off for the life they're destined to share—the dispensation of nutrition. This is why a farmer does everything a farmer must do.

At ummpy Nancy Roe is the woman with the key to my metaphoric potato house, a place where I'm sure to discover the exact definition of the name Aroostook. She is a quiet, competent, bespeckled dumpling of a woman who is filling in as reference librarian on this Saturday, my harvest day at the UMPI library. Her usual job is technical services cataloger, but, with no great stretch of imagination, I can see her aproned and presiding over the scallop-potato tray in the school cafeteria. Unless you are starving, the nurturing of body and mind are coequal in my book. This book. Without Nancy Roe, her key, and her willingness to flex the letter of the library law, I would have missed my potato house.

The Aroostook Room, as it turns out, does have certain quasi esoteric restrictions. It is open only at certain hours on equally certain days and by appointment at other times. This is one of those other times, but I am here without prior appointment because I'm with Nancy Roe. Far from the dank or dim or cement of floor, this room is carpeted and light, with lots of sky drifting by outside the high windows. A shower has passed and the wide rinsed blue, floats tufts of torn cloud. I'm momentarily mesmerized as I turn from the stacks to lollygag over the round table which is currently piled with our finds.

What couldn't a writer do with all this, a transcriber in search of the nutritious all-rounder for the human psyche? It's been said that potatoes are the all-rounders of the vegetable world, containing most every nutrient needed by humankind. They've got just about everything but cholesterol and vitamin A. Only beans, peas, dried seaweed, and spinach soufflé have more protein, according to listings from the University of Maine Cooperative Extension. A scribe searching here would discover that the room is itself the potato equivalent, full of history biography geography geology biology folk stories, poetry, songs, and other logos pertinent to the body of human interest.

Allen is riffling through a periodical published by the Polar Star Association for info on the old Presque Isle air base. He is incidentally unearthing articles on The County's German prisoners of war, on the transatlantic balloon flight, and the first attempt—a decade ago—to close Loring Air Force Base.

I glance through this article myself and find a good quote which might apply today. It seems the formation at that time of the Loring Readjustment Committee "affirmed that the well-being of a region depends on the wisdom of its own people and not on decisions by the federal government." It's a nice quote—a solid sentiment—but I can't help remembering that the base was not built and manned by anybody but the federal government. That it was located strategically—furthest northeast point in the country. The community's labor force and supply will have no one to cater when it's closed.

But I'm getting distracted. What about my interest in defining the meaning of the *word* Aroostook, a word that sticks to the roof of my mouth? Even here, with the combined efforts of Nancy Roe (imagined potato slinger) and myself (would-be potato eater), we are not having the initial success one might expect. There are many fine books on the history and contents of The County, yet the precise origin of its name eludes us.

One source, which mentions that Aroostook is the size of Rhode Island and Connecticut combined, comes close: the name is from a (implied generic?) Native American word meaning "good" or "smooth" water. This must be referring to Aroostook River, which by my map appears to meander and therefore must be thick with sediment, slow flowing, making it smooth.

Now Nancy Roe's eye happens upon a white booklet with black lettering: *Aroostook: the First 60 Years*, by the author of some of my agricultural knowledge, Clarence A. Day. I spent many an hour in his book on the history of Maine Agriculture and now here he is expounding on *The County* alone. I turn a page. Here's Chapter one: "The Name and First Settlement."

The book is a true work of scholarship, for Day has unearthed no less than 18 forms of pronunciation and spelling, plus a few odd names unrelated to the present form. Examples of early forms: Restook, Listook, Oolastook, Wallastook, Aroostic. They are all derived from either Abenaki or Maliseet origins. The first documentation occurred in 1699 when DeRozier applied it to the name of a native settlement of the St. John River near the mouth of the Aroostook River where it empties into that larger flood. Arastuk, DeRozier called it. The meaning was variously fine, good, smooth, beautiful. One form meant "Stream where you get smooth boughs." The sound of it speaks to me archetypically, for water and boughs are primal, mythopoeic.

J.R.R. Tolkien, initially fascinated by linguistic aesthetic qualities, used his invented elvish languages without interpretation in his mythology and heroic romances. He believed that pure utterance, unencumbered by meaning, could speak to our imaginations in much the same way as music. And it's true that our first encounter with language, as babies, is just so. It speaks to our imagination in the form of musical sounds.

My fondness for the word comes first from the way it moves through my mouth. *Aroostook* pushes from my larynx toward the front of my mouth on a long oo sound. It spits past puckered lips only to be pulled back and stuck on my palate. This brings primal memories of childhood, of when I would sit in some quiet nook with my eyes closed, feeling for words and syllables with the inner contours of tongue and mouth: *texture, chunky, smooth*. I'd say them over and over. I would think of the meaning in these sounds and see if the meanings matched the feel of them. Often they did. Yielding up sounds with no perceived meaning is fun. My father made a verbal hash of his daughters' names for the sheer vocal silliness of it. And I've noticed young children seriously at play with it: My child Seth once had *ashy bolp bolp* and *beeka bacca booca* for verbal toys.

The Aroostook Room

Now that I know Aroostook's definitions and its new-to-me vocal forms, the word is enhanced. But here's more: the rich, varied, and fruity *experience* of this land the name will henceforth recall. The sights and histories of potato, caldera and gas balloon; of elms living and dead, of Ohio, and of collapsing picturesque barns. What more's to come I don't yet know, I'm only as far as Presque Isle, as far as the first full day and the ummpy library with Allen, English, and Algonquin for companions.

There's still French, both the language and people, as part of the heritage of Aroostook. There is the sacred and little-known heritage of the Micmacs which I may never learn much about. They're people still quietly with us today, the oldest inhabitants who kept no written records, made no permanent settlements. The strains are part of the diversity of Aroostook which keeps it lively, alive.

In this black and white booklet here in my hands, Day declares that French Acadians were the first Europeans to settle in what would become The County. They had been pioneer-citizen-farmers of Acadia, later called Nova Scotia. Dispossessed by the English, they were forced at gunpoint to leave their homes, fields, woodlands. It was circa 1750, before Yankee Mainers who lived along the coast ever heard of a place called Aroostook. This land and the crown of Maine were settled in secret, by a people fleeing for their lives and making the first permanent settlements. They brought with them a language made more sacred by the hatred of those who persecuted them for it. And so the language was made food for them, nourishing the culture and keeping it alive. It's true: words and food are metaphorically united in their use of the mouth. The precept is underscored by this coupling. The body is comprised of foods we eat, the soul of spoken words.

But Nancy Roe is patiently waiting, key in hand. And we, obliged strangers who've come to root among these books, must humbly remember that she is. In a flurry we gather up what we have and cart it downstairs to the photocopier on the main floor.

Broccoli Bombers

Little to break the northern gales on this vast flat land, with views as from a mountaintop. The sky surrounds us; deep, large with cloud. *The vast Above*. Below is the spread flatland where nothing hinders the north's majestic force. Allen and I are constantly exclaiming over this afternoon's heaven, its ponderous depths and heights. Midday showers are passing, leaving rent clouds, exposing the blue with its levels of light. The monochromatic value scale—of light through dark displayed in clouds—hangs low upon the horizon. As though the people of that place, in distant Limestone, could reach up and touch the base of the scale with hands formed of flesh.

We pass fields of thick stocks and dark leaves: the broccoli fields. This is the crop adopted by some potato farmers in a depressed market. The Caribou loams and Aroostook climate agree with the blue-green florletted vegetable. Maine has become the major broccoli producer behind California, thanks to the proximity of the great Northeast population corridor. The big green plant helped nudge The County's agricultural industry into economic balance during the mid-to-late 1980s. But I don't look for broccoli to overhaul Aroostook's basic monocultural industry (even though it does vastly overtop potatoes in vitamin A). Popular taste decrees that potatoes will forever out-produce broccoli.

We are approaching Caribou. This first tour of town is a brief one as we slip through and are on our way again. Turning off route 1 onto 89, we travel eastward toward the international borderland. There, distantly, we see a long gray cloud sifting great sheets of rain on the vast autumnal land.

Signs seen along the road: *Seven Types of Bear Lure. New potatoes 10 lbs., $1.50. Loring Air Force Base*, with arrow pointing left. Let's just pop up to the base and see if we can see any B-52's. I'd like to see that example of the Vietnam War vetern's aerial savior, the mainstay of American air

Broccoli Bombers

power since the 1950s. Anti-ship missiles, cruise missiles, gravity bombs, sea mines, you name it, these monsters have launched or dropped it, cargo load of death.

Allen pulls into the visitors' lot. A camouflage uniform topped with black beret, steps from the gate house. Allen, a lithe middle-aged man with nimbus of golden white hair, approaches. I watch from the front seat as the guard salutes a passing four-wheel-drive vehicle, and then stands down a bit to answer my spouse. Allen returns with the not unexpected answer that we cannot go on base unless someone vouches for us.

So we are off again upon the "spuds speedway," traveling parallel to the base four miles along two of its sides. Along the way we can observe nothing but trees and brush—hiding the hardware and housing. We see no B-52's. A flip through the old booklet that Allen picked up at the teacher's bookshop tells about the B52Gs and the flying squadrons of the Limestone base. It speaks of two refueling squadrons and the 69th bombardment squadron, which played "a key role in the mission of strategic defense."

In slightly less than one week from this moment of our travels on route 89, the president of the United States (entrenched broccoli hater) will announce the elimination of long-range strategic nuclear weapons. For the first time in 36 years the alert status of the Strategic Air Command will cease. Those fliers who have been living and sleeping but a few feet from the mighty bombers will stand down with relief. Relief in the knowledge that the finger of ultimate destruction will no longer rest, however lightly, upon the trigger. No mean legacy for a president. Jubilation will inflect the flyers' statements to the media, for there has been no rest of flight or spirit for the group since 1955. Always there were engines thrusting; always the heavy bombs within and the mighty outspread wings in flight above the confines of earth. We have been practicing MAD with the Soviet Union—Mutual Assured Destruction. Not only jubilation, but a deep and reverent gratitude is called forth: Yes, the weapons will be with us still, but the conspiracy of MADness between enemies will end. The constant readiness to unleash hidden power, the power of the plutonium atom upon the flesh of all humankind shall cease. For now.

A loaded potato truck lumbers by, heading west. Into the recorder I say: "Allen's idea for the reuse of Loring Air Force Base . . . is for the Salvation Army . . . no (he corrects me) the Red Cross to take over and fly potatoes out to starving people around the world. It would be the Strategic Food Command." Ready on a moment's notice to bomb the hell out of hunger.

We pass a sign pointing the village limit: *Welcome to Limestone. Some of the world's best potatoes, largest bombers and fastest fighters.* (Large bombers is right. These are the stats on the B52G: 488,000 lbs; wingspan 185 ft.; height 40 ft.; thrust per engine 10,000 lbs.. Number of engines: eight. Altitude 50,000 ft. . . . About nine miles into the heavens.)

The sign reveals the town's pride in the base and in its potatoes, though *not* in that order. But apparently the Defense Base Closure and Realignment Commission does not find the feeling mutual. This is evident by looking at the succession of headlines in the *Presque Isle Star-Herald*. Here we see the drama of rejection unfold:

At the end of May readers were informed that "Closure commissioners land at Loring. . . ." In early June readers learned that "Loring impresses visitors." On June 12 the headlines revealed that the "Loring waiting game is on." And on July 3: "Commission cans Loring." The vote was five to two to close the base, "citing an inferior 'quality of life' for service personnel living in Aroostook County."

—?

Rural life may be safer, more beautiful, lacking in crime and tall buildings, but the commission believes only a metropolitan center can provide the diversion necessary "to keep pilots . . . from leaving the Air Force prematurely." This reason falls outside "the eight statutory criteria of the Base Closure Act." By law, closings must be based on tactical and logistical considerations.

The closing will have a significant impact on northeastern Maine, on its economy and population numbers. An estimated 8500 jobs and "152 million and payroll dollars will disappear within three years of the base closing." Four and a half million will evaporate from municipal budgets. 15,000 residents will leave. A 12% hike in electric rates is predicted and property values will nose dive. The sheer scale of the burden is evident elsewhere: the school system will shrink from 1400 students to about 200 and from 177 employees to fewer than 35. . . . these figures are from the article. The town's 6.5 million-dollar high school will close. Said one official, "We will be reduced to a one-room schoolhouse." But, by law, these concerns fall outside the commission's criteria.

Will "quality of life" be diminished by all this loss? Area communities will find out. With apologies for glibness of expression, multiplied by

Broccoli Bombers

tossing around the facts and figures of statistics, I must say: a one-room schoolhouse? Goody.

The sun is out there, intermittently splashing light between the clouds, firing up colors: shimmering greens and yellows, deep dark reds, the searing oranges of changing foliage. We pass more fields of potatoes and broccoli.

One would not ordinarily think of broccoli as a subject or substance of vision. But in a September newsletter of the Good Shepherd Food Bank one finds an account by a broccoli visionary. Located in Lewiston/Auburn, this food bank feeds thousands in Maine and northern New England with food donated by backyard gardeners and major growers and processors. In the last ten years they have distributed 20,000,000 lbs. of food with zero tax dollars. A crowning achievement for fingers and hands formed in flesh.

It doesn't say who wrote the newsletter, *More Than Food*, but the author has visions. Strange visions. When the hush of hunger is embodied in one fifth of the world's people . . . when one billion are at this moment desperately hungry . . . it *takes* vision. However this particular visionary saw broccoli. If it weren't for the Good Shepherd Food Bank's average 2,000,000 lbs. per year distributed one might want to steer clear of this individual.

Even though I know what it is to have empty cupboards, to be hungry enough to pray with my children for food—on our knees beside the sofa in a place called Ohio—and I have rejoiced to have food stamps and eat in a soup kitchen—it must be confessed that my words again fail, degenerate into glibness. In a former entry, I wrote about the Glory of God, about human suffering, and my words seemed appropriate and not so superficial. How is it that I might attempt a description of *Shekhinah* and great suffering without (perhaps?) *great* failure, yet stumble over a description of some lowly visionary?

The spirit and tone are influences. But borrowing is more. In the first instance I borrowed all from the prophet who actually *saw* the Glory of God. He saw, among other aspects of the Glory, "a fire enfolding itself." The closest I've personally come in approximating this was while standing beneath the blinding white afterburners of an F-14 Tomcat as it executed near vertical white-light ascent. Have you felt the seismic shock, witnessed the fused glow of the mushroom cloud? You're closer still. (One's entire attention consumed, all thoughts of self shrivel away.) Thus, words of expression failing me, I borrowed from Ezekiel. Here my problem of glib description of this broccoli visionary won't mend. I know a little of prose and dreams; next to nothing of poetry and visions. I write of "bombing hell out of hunger" because one billion starving people are not in the room with me as I write. My eyes are not watching my children starve. If they were I could not write of it. So my words lack proportion, propriety. Even the title of this piece, "Broccoli Bombers," is facile.

"For several years," writes the anonymous author of *More Than Food*, "I've dreamt of receiving fresh broccoli, grown in the fields of northern Maine. I had heard of all the broccoli left in the fields, and envisioned transporting volunteers the long distance, and physically picking second-grade broccoli and hauling it back to our warehouse in Lewiston."

Oh if we had more such visionaries! Scanning the nutritional value of broccoli, one begins to understand the magnitude of the vision. Yet there is more. Studies soon-to-be published will show that broccoli's *sulforaphene* triggers enzymes that nullify carcinogens. Eating such *cruciferous* vegetables—broccoli cauliflower cabbage brussels-sprouts—lowers the risk of breast, stomach, and bowel cancers.

Broccoli is the true visionary food. Possessed of carotene, it contains a fair amount of vitamin A—2,330 international units—a necessary component in the formation of visual pigments. Night blindness is one symptom of a deficiency in vitamin A. We see carotene blazing off autumnal trees long after chlorophyll is dead and gone. It even remains a while in the leaves when leaves have fallen to earth. Even corn, possessing less than one tenth broccoli's carotene, has *some* content which the liver can process for visual pigments.

But no volunteers were transported to Aroostook, no second-grade broccoli was picked and hauled to Lewiston. Then, admitting failure, one day the visionary spoke to our commissioner of the Maine Department of Agriculture, Bernard Shaw. " 'I can do that for you.' " Then they connected to Bud Ayers with Maine Packers Inc., who did more than the visionary visualized. They received abundant broccoli fresh, not second-grade, from these fields. The writer also recounted efforts of some Bates College students to preserve thousands of pounds for winter distribution.

We have come into the borderlands as seen earlier in this piece from a distance. We've come to that land beneath the moving skyscrape where we might've expected to reach into clouds and touch the base of the monochromatic value scale, lifted in layers of dark and light. Some hands of flesh would thrust glibly toward heaven, sheathed in metal and breathing fire: vaulting and thunderous, with wingspans as broad as a field of broccoli.

Other hands lie slack in starvation, palms upward, curled and hopeless in silky dust.

Oh but these hands are deftly formed. Deftly formed. All these hands of dust.

The Borderland

ON OUR WAY OUT of Presque Isle we crossed the Aroostook River for the first time, seeing some of the character of its "smooth good water." Its shallow body lay very green under curving banks, its sources faraway westward beyond rolling county lands, county lines. Deep beyond artificial borderlands in the midst of the state, Good Smooth Water begins at a convergence of Munsungan and Millinocket Streams. This is near the shared border of Piscatiquis and Penobscot Counties, about 60 km southwest of Presque Isle as the raven flies. Its route is tortuous and long, the river gaining in volume as it winds northeastward through The County; Aroostook traverses valley and bog on its way to the wider St. John, the watery international borderline.

The Androscoggin—our river in Western Maine—drains part of the most elevated portions of the state, southward into the Gulf of Maine. The St. John River, running 211 miles, drains the state's massive Eastern Upland region. It provides a mutual border with Canada, decreed in 1842, before tensions could bring a full-fledged war between the US and Great Britain. The Aroostook, arising in T8-R8 (Township 8, Range 8) winds seventy five miles, draining the land eastward through Presque Isle, Caribou, and Fort Fairfield. There it crosses the artificial borderline. At Aroostook Junction in New Brunswick it joins the St. John. The St. John brings all these waters into the Gulf of Maine by way of New Brunswick, Canada.

The Aroostook River is a floodplain body, its drainage pattern differing from patterns that arise in mountains. Such rocky places aren't uniformly resistant. Here, on this floodplain, rivers flow long, gentle and northeast-treading through folds in bedrock, as Kendall describes. In broad valleys there is room to meander. The stream makes its bed by removing soil in its quicker passage along the outside berms above its curves. Inside the curve the stream flows more slowly, dropping sediments and building sandbars.

Thus the water takes from one side and gives to the other, back and forth across the floodplain. A floodplain gains ground, building rich bottomland suitable for farming. The nature of these sediments is limey, possessing a balanced pH that is perfect for potatoes.

Approaching the village of Limestone in the international border country, we see a warning sign: moose crossing. And yet again another potato truck, with black plywood cover clamped over it. There lie the scattered woodlands and bright homes of Limestone dotting the area. Where's the town's village? We pass a graveyard, St. Louis Cemetery. The settlement is coming into view. Many white houses line a sweet foliaged curve in the distance. And there a stream called Limestone runs through.

Here's Main Street—Kelly's Gun Shop, Gervais Movie Rentals, at $.99; Exxon and Irving. A broad thoroughfare with white buildings, children running and skipping. Groceries pizza auto-parts. Tri-community recycling. It's rural America. Its Iowa, Kansas and Minnesota; Ohio.

Four-sixteen p.m., slightly more than 24 hours since leaving the Western Mountains, and we here on Route 18, traveling north along the St. John toward Van Buren and supper. The valley is wide, this floodplain. It speaks of the floodplain which is History.

After bitter strife between the US and Great Britain, bringing them onto the berm of war, the shining body paralleling our route was finally designated to divide things colonial and English from things independent and American. For some time before that, this border question wasn't receiving the attention in the federal legislature that most Mainers thought it deserved. To the federal government it was, according to Charles E. Clark in *Maine: a History*, only one difference with Britain needing diplomacy. But Maine had fire, gumption, *and a cannon*; she had a daring martyr in John Baker, who was jailed in New Brunswick for raising an American flag. And she had the political argument of states' rights.

This was the state's reason for rejecting a compromise negotiated by the King of the Netherlands in which the proposed boundary was set further north than presently. Maine *would have had* a more sizable chunk of valuable timberland and the northern portion of the St. John to herself. But Maine balked, Maine wanted more. After nearly two decades of fuss and increase of armaments, the state finally settled, perhaps out of weariness and the application of cash. The boundary dispute, owing to history's leveling floodplain, took from one side and gave to the other.

Visiting the Eastern Uplands

Over the wide river we see today's Canada, New Brunswick and its towns of Martin, Bellefleur, and L'Eglise. The river is broad, broader than our Androscoggin. Its tiny towns, diminished by perspective, are alternately shining and shadowed. I recognize churches in miniature, but solid, and impressive, even in the distance. Land there is shorn and turned into garden, where once it was filled with immense solemn wind-riffled trees.

The fair land of this valley, now so productive of food, was once in forest bough upon bough; dark mountainous trees having trunks five and six feet through. How did it become so smooth and wide of sky? If a man, like an ant, could stand beside a living coniferous monster and think to fall it . . . whatever gave him the idea? With crosscut saw and another man he would consider it workable, but getting it to market was something else. Here, alongside our route, is the reflecting body that made them think they could do it. This St. John, its tributaries surging in spring, draining this rolling land, brought ancient trunks to market for trespassers.

Here at this boundary the war for timber was waged in hustle, in water and sweat; in theft. For prior to and after the culmination and settling of the border dispute by the Webster-Ashburton Treaty in 1842, trespassers of both countries were busy dismantling the forest. Since an earlier time when Europeans usurped the northeast, both public and the private holdings of proprietors were plundered by the insatiable saws of lumbermen. They paid crews to sever the trees from their moorings and wrestle them downstream. The forest was so vast, its waterways so far-reaching, that anyone with a commanding personality and a particular disregard for the laws or legal rights of others could be a lumbermen. Even government officials. Richard G. Wood, in his *Lumbering in Maine, 1820–1861*, cites evidence of a county commissioner who had his own crew in the woods.

Think of the effort it took to remove stumps left behind (stumps described as large enough to hold a yoke of oxen), in order to achieve the smoothness and care visible today. The distant fields are no longer nubbly with large stumps, like stumble on the face of *The County* after its shave. One account told of shared fields—fields where grain grew between these hulking stumped remnants.

Van Buren comes up to the roadside in dwellings and buildings. We ease into a parking space beside a row of storefronts and get out to stretch, and look around. It's a brisk late afternoon; fresh, spotted with rain. And we are hungry.

The Borderland

We walk along the row of shops and come to a gap in buildings. Look out across the river toward the foliaged embankment and above, where the French-Canadian town of St.-Leonard rises. Wind blows through the gap upon us, cold and forceful, fiercely fresh. Out of St.-Leonard a great pillar of rainbow ascends, descends. The colors—at first grading into one another—grow more vivid and defined as we watch. Violet blue green yellow orange and red. These refractions and reflections shine out brightly from solid earth and its town, jutting into vaporous cloud above. Tiny buildings are set beneath, the shimmering harbinger in their midst. The bright bow is skewered with a church spire, surmounted by thin tenuous cross.

Transfixed we watch, scoured by cold wind. But our attention wavers in the chill blast. Colors dim and fade. They are gone into gray. We turn and go back to get coats.

Following our meal at a restaurant where old women converse in French and the waitress asks our orders in accented English, we take the road and bridge across the St. John into another country. At the border-crossing station a guard looks at us, at our IDs, and asks a few questions. He politely says pull the car over, park and come inside. The French-Canadian guard still has our licenses. Perhaps Allen's appearance—his hair was short when the picture was taken and has since grown out—poses doubts about us?

We sit in the lobby on hard chairs, waiting judgment from the back room. I fidget, stand, peruse nearby racks of flyers. There are pamphlets in both English and French: one side says *Entrer au Canada pour etudier ou travailler*. I flip it over and turn it upside down, reading, *Entering Canada to study or work*. Delighted, I show Allen. An officer in the room with us watches me. He asks why we have come over to St.-Leonard. I tell about being a writer, about studying Aroostook and following the American road along the St. John. I smile like a sheep in telling of how a rainbow suggested the change of road. We plan now to travel Canadian route 2 through French New Brunswick to Edmunston, and there cross the river back into Maine at Madawaska.

"Ah, but not all rainbows are in Canada," he answers, no doubt hoping to ward off a prolonged visit by old hippies.

"Yes. . . . We have them over in Maine." I smile. (Again like a sheep).

Geology makes its own countries and sets its own borders. After a night in St.-Leonard, we begin traveling the foggy TransCanada highway. Coming

Visiting the Eastern Uplands

out upon gentle ridges into streaming sunlight, we see that the unfolding landscape is like that of Aroostook. Our course now parallels the St. John River along the eastern shore, looking across upon that other nation, county and state. But its soil and topography is that of Canada. The St. John takes soil from New Brunswick, gives it to Maine, and vice versa. In this valley there are not two geological countries, but one.

Yet, linguistically and culturally this is another country. For signs are all bilingual, we were waited on this morning by people bilingual. Is it the same on the other side of the gently sloping vale? Signs there are all in English. Maine, then, does not as much acknowledge its French heritage. For years it was suppressed by bigotry. Today we have festivals honoring things French, but still no signs in French. Language, the authentic presence of the culture, is slighted.

Yet we do have a shared history of bigotry. Both Anglo and French cultures dispossessed something ancient and harmonious which was here before they came (although, arguably, the French did better by them). Native ecological heritage was a more sacred way of life, for it took what was needed for survival and joy from a land large in trees, with little or no thought of rapacious gain.

For 200 years the Micmacs have made baskets of black and brown ash in order to eke out their subsistence. Find, fall, trim, peel, says *Our Lives in Our Hands* by Bunny McBride. A trunk will be heavily pounded with the blunt side of the ax, causing separation along layering growth rings which as strips can then be woven. Paradoxically the skill was learned from immigrant Northern Europeans, and perfected by the natives. These quiet people have helped bring in the Maine traditional harvest of potato and blueberry, they hunt, search swamps for ash suitable to weave these patinaed works of art and handcraft. There is season, cycle, and ritual to their work as well as great skill. Such lives have poetry and power many of us Anglos will never know.

The ridges roll away beneath our wheels. Great white tufts of vapor straddle the river where valleys of tributary streams intersect. Ridges of earthbound cloud extend into Aroostook County with mighty disregard for border crossings and nationalities. This Canadian side of the river seems more concerned with civilization, appears more populous and less forested. Its churches are massive, imposing and ponderous. Elegant, and a weight upon earth. Across river the Yankee churches are tiny and white, light and clapboard, austere within. A flood could carry one down the street to a new location. A glimpse of Maine's French history shows a church with strong grip upon its parishioners, ponderous structures interiorly echoing an imposition in every aspect of their lives. It calls language paramount, saying, "lose your language, lose your faith." How can you be French and Catholic if you no longer speak French?

St. Anne. Elms line drives or dot the roads. Settlements pass, signs. *Rivierre-Verte. St. Basile.*

Edmunston/Madawaska, mill towns. Edmunston on this Canadian side of the border/river. A hilly twin city, reminding me of French cultural Lewiston/Auburn which straddles the Androscoggin. Similarities do not end with appearances, for both Twin communities drew the French as mill-town magnets. But this mill town is rooted in two different nations.

New glamorous buildings, an arena, putt-putt, old buildings, a massive stone church with twin spired towers. The cemetery with rows like wheat of shining pink or black graven headstones. Allen calls it stylish. One uses the word cemetery, not graveyard, in token of this. The French of anything, even graves, is seldom less than elegant.

We come to the bridge, the river, the international border. But first, here's a shop you won't find on the other side—with goods and regulations of an unusual nature in other contexts. Here we stop to try and collect a refund on tax paid on our motel room last night and discover it's not worth the effort. Allen and I see firsthand one reason why Canadian dissent on taxes is strong. The shop attendant oversees sales of shelf contents: floor to ceiling, yards and yards of fine liquors, coolers of beer and ale, wines. Myriad cartons of cigarettes and tobacco products. All for duty-free purchase, *if* you are crossing the bridge. This is how government saves its people from lung and heart disorders, and from the destruction of alcoholism. Since the government pays for health care of its citizens, heavy taxes on these items help offset the cost of paying for these diseases. Why provide all this for those leaving the nation, for those entering the *other* nation?

There is now not a land without history, the written word. And borderlands have more history than others. Here in this river valley the lives of some humans play themselves out in getting—in ravaging nature's body apace. And here others, having escaped rejection, clear the leavings to make productive and habitable what remains. This is history fraught with struggle. But do we learn anything, as historians insist we must?

Some learn that their ancestors were abused, dispossessed; and that their oppressors may have something to bequeath them. Others find wrongs unaddressed festering to yield a brutal bitterness. Borders *can* come into contention, strife rekindling and burgeoning—strife knowing no borders or bounds. But this is the way of meandering rivers. The flood passes by, curving. It takes from one side and gives to the other. Back and forth, giving-and-taking, across the broad floodplain.

Industry on the Borderline

ANTOINE DE SAINT-EXUPERY, THE heroic French aviator, crashed into the Mediterranean Sea en route from a World War II reconnaissance mission—in one of the marvelous machines of his age. Flying a P-38 through gunfire, fragile in air, he went down into eternity. He had written that the machine at first seemed a way of separating man from nature's great problems but truly plunged man deep into them.

Should we hate machines? We'd have to hate our eyeballs if we did. I'd have to disown the marvelous mechanisms of my own being. Saint-Exupery meant we ought to love machines. We ought to love paper mills. We've got to care enough about the things we invent to invent them right, and do right with what we invent. Why don't we care enough for our factories, the work of our ingenuity, to build what is safe, pleasant, and harmonious to its surroundings and workers? Why? Why isn't genius and engineering, if it *is* genius and engineering, thus employed?

Upon crossing back into the states at Madawaska, Maine, Allen and I see the massive cylindrical storage tanks and ponderous buildings of the Paper Company, an international venture. Stock, made from pulped trees, is pumped across the St. John from Edmunston, Canada to this mill, where it is made into paper. Madawaska rises above the river and above the mill, in concrete, aluminum, glass, wood and brick. Driving up hill we see sides of a dirty industrious river valley. Across the way, high hazy colored foliage of Edmunston, Canada is glimpsed through gaps in buildings. There are no bilingual signs here, yet the so-called second-language is evident in the French names appearing over shops and services. The main thoroughfare up here is adorned with beautiful old-fashioned street lamps—evidence of taste. Ornate black poles uplifting frosted glass globes, etched, and banded with gold filigree. At night, when darkness hovers just out of reach, and

Visiting the Eastern Uplands

steam pours up from below, lit by the eerie pink-orange of the mill's sodium vapor lamps, these elegant streetlamps must cast an opposing romantic glow along the avenue. On two corners there are lamps with four globes each, as though great candelabrums.

We pull up in front of Bridge Street Restaurant, just above the steaming mill on a hillside full of shops and apartments. Coffee time. I look down toward the foot of the hill at the bridge leading back to metropolitan Canada. Getting out of the car we hear the rumbling of paper dryers below. Familiar sound, especially to Allen. Vast hot clouds billow into the cleft between these hill towns flanking the St. John. Inside is a roaring paper machine, about the length of a football field, winding a 30-foot wide sheet of paper. The clouds come off this paper, which begins as a sheet of 99% water moving on wire mesh. The sheet moves down the length and then through dryers, losing the water to become a body of paper, shooting out toward great rollers where it's wound at a maddening pace. An hour's break in production can lose as much as $50,000 in our late 1980s production time.

As I look out upon the mills, Allen says this particular company has been squabbling over OSHA fines for unsafe conditions. There is a sign, on the side of a building I can see from here, proclaiming the safety slogan of the month. Below, where this month's slogan should be posted, is an empty brick wall.

It's not surprising that paper production, when practiced on this scale, is unsafe. The surprise would be if it were not unsafe. One factor contributing to the industry's accident rate is a thoroughgoing disregard of human biology's circadian rhythm. In backward rotating shift-work, workers are given what amounts to four days to recover from an unnatural and fatiguing schedule . . . before said schedule starts over again: Work seven nights, have a day off and come back to work on the afternoon shift for another seven days, have a day off and return in the morning for seven days. Doing this to the human form is asking for accidents. The worker is fuzzy-headed and unsettled, without the edge needed to work safely around monstrous booming machinery.

Around the turn of the 20th-century, French-Canadian immigrants began coming to papermaking towns in Maine. Genius had invented machinery to turn wood fiber into paper. Towns built themselves overnight around the hungry machines. Mills devoured the forests around them and reached out for more. They were constructed on rivers—for power generation, log transportation, and because paper begins on the wet-end . . . as a flow of water with a dab of pulp. Rivers were also used to flush effluent downstream. Because investment confers power on genius, it took genius to degrade the pure drainage of one million green acres into an open sewer full of dangerous chemicals. Why doesn't genius love its work enough to perfect it before going into full-scale production? Why can't it see a river full of chemicals as a defect in its design?

Wendell Berry—conservation essayist, farmer, and creative writer—wrote that for all our inventiveness, we can imagine ourselves only so far into the future before we get into serious trouble. Then problems accrue which we hadn't imagined. Man can and did imagine the old-growth forests right out of this land, but he cannot imagine them back into it anytime soon.

This particular river valley is fortunate.

The limey nature of soil in this borderline land will see to it that here there may always be food. Owing to thoroughgoing disregard of biology, and of Saint-Exupery's "great problem of nature," many other lands are not so fortunate. Once their old growths are taken away by machinery, once they have gone over that line, the land will be able to give them nothing more. Lands hot and steamy and gloriously green—their soils can produce wholly fecund, diverse, and elegant jungle sufficient to every need. Or—clear-cut—they can produce nothing at all.

The Excesses and Economies of Travel

ENTERING THE BRIDGE STREET Restaurant in Madawaska, we find the air thick with the language of French. Yet it's a small place with few patrons this midmorning. A high corner room with a view of the steaming mill below and foliaged streets of Edmunston rising across the gorge. We sit in a corner booth on high-backed wooden benches, looking out. The trestle table has curved supports and a red Formica top. Coffee, served by a Frenchwoman, tastes different. Allen describes it as chocolaty. We sit and study the map together, ignorant, but half aware of the romantic and undulant flow of speech. Those beautiful tripping utterances with (to us as to babes) no discernible meanings.

The route from here to Frenchville to Fort Kent is plain. It shall be route 1, in red, which terminates at Fort Kent. But from there, where? We hash it over. Then, "Do what you want," says Allen. "It's your trip."

I want to return to Caribou and Presque Isle. At Caribou I missed a good example of dipping thinly bedded limestone, mentioned in Kendall's book. Limestone, I've written here, is a significant foundation in Aroostook. And I want more information on potatoes, obtainable at the Cooperative Extension in Presque Isle. So we must visit those two towns before we head home. But, by what route?

The map shows two, 161 and 11. The former is punctuated with French names—Daigle, Ouelette, Guerette—and some lakes; it is most direct. The latter is a roundabout way, with English names and some lakes. But it is more remote. on the edge, thereby intriguing me. The edge is my word for the boundary between the big woods of the western Aroostook and its orderly farm country of the east. The edge is the hem of the Great Forest, trimming the rolling plain of farms . . . which edges, in its turn, the aisle of civilization that borders the St. John. A border within a border within a border. The world is all borders and boundaries. We are always on the edge of some other place.

But, in this particular body of Maine, forest is the core edged by everything else. Great as it is in its farmland, Aroostook—I should tell you—is mostly woodland, trees.

We are purring through Frenchville, and we have a wide blue day after pearly early fog. The air is mild, the valley of St. John in foliage at the height of autumn's last light. Frenchville is a settlement in the midst of combined woodland/farmland; we see clearcuts on ridges in Canada, across the international border, as we drive. These clearcuts appear as variegated crew cuts in the billowy tresses of standing timber. This section of river valley rounding the curve of the northern crown of Maine, is steeper, almost mountainous compared to the rolling Ohio-lands we saw southward earlier.

We rise slowly through the low village of Frenchville. Reaching the outskirts, we are about to step it up, skip along, when sight of a peculiar wooden structure arrests us. "What is it?" I asked, gaping upward.

"It's an old railroad water tower." Allen reads from a sign: "Frenchville Historical Society. Bangor and Aroostook Railroad."

Lined up beside tracks are tiny depot, rust-red caboose, and this massive charcoal-green water tank—freshly stained, its trestle trued up. We pull onto the gravel and climb out to look around. This is the old Frenchville train station and water tank for steam locomotion. Dwarfing us, it's made of vertical slats wrapped with cable and secured by old-fashioned screw turnbuckles. The construction reminds me of a gigantic barrel. Its roof is a shingled octagon with pointy apex.

Walking around to the back we notice a trough extending from the tank. The old steam locomotive would pull up here and get water for its boiler. The boiler would be stoked with wood or coal—steam pressure driving heavy pistons to turn massive steel wheels.

If the St. John gave our first lumber barons to imagine they could get giant trees out of the woods, these are the museum pieces that made Aroostook's farmers imagine they could survive and prosper on a single crop. The Bangor and Aroostook Railroad was not the first through *The County*; there were the Canadian Railway and the short-lived European and North American Railroad. But the B&A was the one to connect Aroostook with the rest of Maine, and its lucrative coastal and shipping ventures. Prior to 1895 *The County* contented itself with a more diversified produce, namely wheat, oats, buckwheat and grass seed to mention the most prominent. It was the iron monster's ability to transport the weightier, bulkier potato crop at efficient speed and cost turning farmers to monoculture. And to monoculture's inherent ups and downs, its bent toward collapse. There's a history of tongue-clucking aimed at Aroostook's farmers. Two of my former college professors, one a historian the other a geographer, have commented on what they called the potato farmer's obstinacy.

Still, with the possibility of frost in every month of the short growing season, successful crops *are* limited. And Charles E. Clark in his *Maine: a History* is a little kinder, likening the potato farmer to the frontiersman.

Allen and I walk back along the caboose, climb its iron stairs and peek through the glass. The doorknob rattles in my hand. Locked. Looking through a small glass pane down its length, we see three bunks at the far end. My gaze moves forward to an old-fashioned ceramic sink under windows. Across from this sits a wooden desk with manual typewriter—next to a wood stove. Sitting forward a bit are a couple coach seats with curtains drawn back. I crane my neck to see beneath my nose where the table with guest register stands. A sign above proclaims the historical society. Hats, $5; buttons, $1; shirts, $7; patches, $4; offerings of life membership to the Frenchville Historical Society. Allen and I are refreshed by it all. The caboose represents domesticity, history, travel, and—to us—work. I'm dreaming now. Oh what a life we could live riding the rails in this!

In writing books about Maine, I have begun in the western part where we live, then gone beyond to see other locales in what some might think a swift and cursory manner. For us it's a large expense, and there's the danger of superficiality and glibness being found in the harvest of words. I try to avoid this by studying places I visit in the work of others, by attentive observation, and by spending time and care over these words. Even so, I make mistakes, and I'm not an authority on anything I write about.

Turning away from our glimpse of the interior, my hand goes to cold iron—a wheel. It looks like a steering wheel, instrument of control. Allen says it's a brake, and climbs down to investigate the undercarriage.

All this iron and steel and steam. The mass, power, pent energy. The opposing weight and wispiness: for steam is but vapor, almost like spirit. But under great pressure there is great power. These two diverse elements came together more than a scant two centuries ago, setting us on the route of industrial and technological progress. The inspired geniuses of science and engineering haven't looked back since.

The Excesses and Economies of Travel

Should they? If they would just look around, even. Look at the once beautiful, lush, thriving and healthful pockets in earth, now polluted, stripped of supporting wildlife. Look at the harmless innocents, natives, who must live in them still. Let genius look toward the future and ask if it truly knows the end of its work.

And me (aside from the genius part), just how am I different from any of this, running along back and forth over boundaries, chasing after *what* with my internal combustion engine, purring and roaring? Zipping through strange, half-familiar communities, knowing little, searching for knowledge, carbon-loading the atmosphere while chasing the metaphor? Dragging my husband up to *The County* after spuds when they are harvested just the other side of the Androscoggin River where we live?

Stooping, Allen finds the brake chain beneath, traveling the length of the car. Imagine turning this iron wheel with the strength of your tiny arms. Imagine stopping a runaway iron monster with bare hands; feeling the opposing muscle fibers in your torso.

Upper Frenchville. Neat, French style brick homes. A church of square hewn colored stones. The country, the shallow upper St. John on our right. Brown flora, drying shrubs line the roadside. Leaves are a dark ravaged green. Pale colors, sere; russets, drying leaves on stocks. Furry goldenrod, gone by. Fall grasses with rattling heads, gone by. Dried stiffened asters. Heavy-headed sunflowers, disks sagging, surrounded by loud yellow petals. Fields of dried autumnal plants full of seed.

Equinox has come and gone, leaving us seeds as the north turns away from light, as life sinks back into roots, exhausted. Colista Morgan, Western Maine author who taught in the one-room school, writes that the plans for next summer are in those seeds. Unless you're a farmer with seed crop, you probably equate seeds with that other Equinox, six months hence. Avid gardeners think of them in January and February while dreaming over pictures of green-blue, carrot yellow, or snowy white in glossy catalogs. Whatever we may think of seeds, next year's food is planned and packed in them. On that one night the darkness is equal in length to its corresponding day. Our mood should be a balanced one, fruitful of gratitude. Floating on its axis, spinning with great speed, earth celebrates the heavenly gesture by giving generously of life.

Fort Kent passing. A little depot; a train restoration project. Riding down Main Street on a bustling Sunday morning. Mass. The church with ornate, shining, wrought iron spire, its tracery depicting leaves, grape clusters, sheaves of wheat. Below are the great white doors of the church. Parishioners issue like seeds tumbling from a gourd, having ingested the body and blood of Christ. They cluster, or climb into their cars to empty the parking lot. One edges his vehicle toward the roadway, eager to be on his way. His license plate catches my eye. A Maine license complete with lobster, one of those vanity plates. *Lichen*, it says.

Driving this busy street, scarcely noticing, we cross an alder-lined tributary of the St. John. The Fish River, according to *The Maine Atlas and Gazetteer*. The Fish River is fifty miles long, connecting three great lakes—Portage, St. Froid, and Eagle—draining them into the St. John here at Fort Kent. Within the limestone cradle of the drainage lie more than two hundred lakes.

We drive on through the bustle, past low buildings and businesses. Here's another bridge over the St. John; a green erector-set bridge on piers, with arches in triplicate. A sign for the border crossing says, "Welcome to Historic Fort Kent. This marks the beginning of US Route 1, ending in Key West, Florida, 2209 miles south."

A brief circuit around the green swarded University of Maine at Fort Kent. In brick. Again, a campus with stretching room—though it is a small college. A place of knowledge on the edge of Maine and its wilderness. Upon these borders of everything, sandwiched like meat between the twin hefty loaves of forest and farmland.

Allen says it's good to have someplace like this in a rural community to give people something to—

"—to broaden themselves."

"—No. To broaden their horizons."

"Looks like we're leaving French country," says Allen. (Perhaps mistakenly.)

"Leaving for . . . what? For where?"

For the edges of the great Northern Maine woods. For Eagle Lake. We are on our rolling route—route 11 toward Eagle Lake and lunch. Broad ridges and long neat fields, woodlands, settlements. TV antennas and satellite dishes, receivers of signals for language and images. Here's inspired travel: sit in bed and go anywhere electronically. How many channels can we get served upon our heavenly-placed satellite dishes? When viewed at once flipping idly through, we see a bright welter, flickering. Multiplicity shoots past flexing irises, into image-focusing lenses toward pigmented

The Excesses and Economies of Travel

receptors. Image-bearing photons trigger signals through to the back of the brain were sight is yielded up to interpretation by the mind. As we idly flip ... flip ... flip. This is how we bring the great city, bright Babylon weltering, into the sacred courts of the mind.

Come out into the country. Come to Eagle Lake for lunch.

Approaching the rest area that overlooks Soldier Pond. We pull up before a green lawn shot with yellow dandelions, and unlimber from the car. Unlimber from the morning's drive through borderlands. Here's a high panoramic view. I look out, breathless from the sweep of wind and distance-blue expanse.

The text for this view, and for the route, is on the signboard above my head. I tilt back and read: *The Aroostook and Fish River Roads*. . . . Ah yes, the Fish River: "The northern portion of present-day route 11, from Sherman to Fort Kent, was planned and constructed in many stages, from 1826 to the 1850s. . . ." Only the rivers made access possible, made claim to the land likely during the border dispute with England. But the road made settlement possible and development of farming and timberlands inevitable, helping to shape the state's boundaries and sustaining activities to this day.

Between two halves of the text runs a wavy line. It depicts route 11 running north from Sherman Station through Patten; running through Marsadis, Ashland, Eagle Lake and on up to Fort Kent on the St. John. By 1839 the road was open, if poor, and money for repair was lacking until years later. "The road," wrote Captain Lucian Webster, "is through the dense forest designated by the trees being felled and the streams roughly bridged, and without a single human habitation or shelter of any kind. Because of tremendous snowstorms and extreme degree of cold there will be great exposure and risk of lives of express riders and of persons bringing through supplies."

Imagine.—Can we in our glutted electron-transport state? . . . Imagine the effort to make the Fish River Road: crosscut sawing the huge timber, heaving out the glacial boulders with timber-pole levers and oxen or draft horses, smoothing the terrain with horse-drawn rollers, paving with sand and gravel and corduroy logs. What would be the non-glib comparison between such an effort and—*flip flip flip*?

After reading the sign I walk down toward one end of the dandelion clearing to take a wider look eastward out across the valley. There lies the curved sheen of Soldier Pond, a wide place in the Fish River. A ridge rises beyond the pond, encrusted in changing foliage. Turning, I see a settlement strung out upon the Road. Could this have been the site of winter shelter long ago? Or would shelter be in a low spot, nestled away out of the sweep of winds (so keen even now on this autumn day). Below me the slope grades down in cover of bushes and young trees, firs and rustling hardwoods. I would shelter in a south-facing curve beneath evergreens, away from the open expanse of Soldier Pond.

As I look outward, beside me Allen says this is the epitome of Northern Maine, thrust up as it is on three sides into another nation. We breathe the cool living breath of wind. This air is coming from some other country. If it blows from west, from north, from east, it is blowing from Canada now. When it pushes up from south, from the great polluted Atlantic seaboard, it comes from our own country. Today it circulates cleanly from northern regions, washing us whole—nostrils, lungs, pores.

Fields across the way are sere, brown, plowed. They've been dug up, their potatoes taken; or was it a buckwheat crop?

We brush through sparse settlements traveling this long road, this west-flanking ridge stretching for miles. Eagle Lake in that distance, seen from above. On the map we see it long and narrow, with a dogleg. Drawing nearer we see sparkling blue water, wide. The car dips down past vertically bedded shaley-looking road cuts. We turn off into Plaisted, on the northern shore.

"House for sale. I'll take it."

"Me, too."

Turning down here rings Allen's bell. That's what I like about him: He's got bells.

Back up to the Fish River Road. A log yard. Logging operation with skidder, silent on Sunday. Loggers keeping it holy, resting. The ridge rises away on the right, covered with trees, a mixed forest. Tall thin trees. Small diameters. Blue blue water opposite. *Welcome to beautiful Eagle Lake.*

Another rest area, high. Remotely it overlooks a shapely curve in the body of the lake. Another sign, more text about the Fish River Road.

> In October, 1839, Gervis reported the results of his road building work. "I came through the road which had been completed from the mouth of the Fish River, Fort Kent, to the Aroostook in company with a Madawaska settler in his wheeled carriage, a French caleche. The route was performed with ease and without the slightest accident. From this day then may be dated the opening of the

fine valley of the St. John to the rest of the State, from which until now it has been separated by an impassable barrier of 45 miles of unbroken forest."

This route we've taken from Madawaska to Eagle Lake encompasses the excesses and economies of our travels. It's a route through technological history, the young history of the ancient land Aroostook. Its inhabitants traveled the gamut through hardship and ease: by foot, horseback, carriage, iron and steam; by the internal combustion engine of Subarus and their like. Without leaving living rooms, citizens travel on signals sent through air, served up on dishes to wherever imagination will ultimately and unforeseeably lead.

Here in *The County* the seeds are dried and waiting. Each with encoded instructions for the next harvest in its cradle of nutrients, ready to pass on its own message of life.

Where Eagles Feed

WE'VE HEARD THE JOKE about Eagle Lake. It's that menu from the Roadkill Restaurant. Porcupine, squirrel, skunk. . . . Someone at the mill showed a menu to Allen before we left on our trip. Roadkill, according to Maine's Humble Farmer, writer Robert Skoglund, is one first-rate economic indicator: If on your commute you pass the same roadkill coming and going, then things aren't too bad. Even when times are good and you happen across a hit-and-run partridge, you'd be wise to take it home for sauteing. Eagles eat fresh roadkill. Keep your eyes open for eagles, wings folding, talons extended. There you'll find fresh meat.

Eagle Lake was named the same year the Fish River Road opened, in 1839, "when Penobscot County Sheriff, Hastings Strickland, camped nearby and observed bald eagles around the lake." Here my mate and I are parked on a ridge above a land burgeoning with wildlife, fit habitat of eagles. Perched high over a gleaming great lake, reading this text, I can understand why Sheriff Strickland's observation occasioned the name. (Though, glancing far into that distance, I'm seeing no eagles.)

From this site the sheriff may have watched mighty mating rituals. These have inspired humans since humans first saw. If only Allen and I could witness the male and female (one third again as large) rolling and diving, flaring off thermals from earth's weighty sides. There were no tribes of our fathers and mothers that did not glory in their remorseless flight. Species of eagles girdled the earth, and everywhere the archetype was revered. When Africans and Anglo-Saxons were primitives, the eagle was a role model and sacred figure. The swift plummet to earth, the mighty swooping to lift its own nurture. . . . It was the inspiration of Celts, Romans, and Native Americans; of Hebrews and Persians and Huns. Of all our fierce ancestors from whose loins we have spilled and spread.

Today we might admire the vision of eagles, but as for mating there'd be none if we did have such vision. If we could see as well as eagles see, we'd see our intended beautifully, in the distance coming the miles, but on closing there would be revulsion. Allen would look at me with eagle eyes and see a zillion cracks in my epidermis: he'd number every hair, note my scalp's holes, its monstrous multitude of follicles. Gazing into my eyes he'd see straight through the vitreous jelly and down, perhaps, into the ganglion flashing. If he could see right into me, my internal workings, he wouldn't like it.

If we could see as eagles see—telescoping and microscoping—we'd have no trouble locating our food. With such vision, seeing even the sun-surrounding rain circle, maybe we'd recognize angels in air. We'd see what cannot now be transmitted by our optic nerves.

We've arrived at remote Eagle Lake, another settlement along the way, not so tiny as those upon the Fish River Road. Eagle Lake Grocery and Liquor Store. TJ's Market. Yard sale. Turkey shoot. Whirligigs on sale in someone's yard. New saltbox apartments in blocks—government-subsidized—overlooking the lake. Older white houses lining the streets.

"Ham radio operator."

"What kind of antennae's that?"

"A quad of some sort."

Down by the railroad tracks we pass freight cars on a siding. Many are full of logs to be sent away, no value adding for the material or jobs for the community. There's a marina. We are hungry for lunch, and stopping here.

A marina—with wood mill separator and blower on top? The Old Mill Marina is a converted wood-turning mill. Allen explains the mechanics of separators, which work by forcing air and wood chips through pipes. The air blows out the top and chips fall down dry into the fuel bin. More incongruities: the windsock turning above, a guide to fly-by floatplanes? Look: show windows display gleaming snowmobiles.

"Arctic highways" is what our son calls the pristine trails of Aroostook. Seth plans soon to own one of these whining polluters—something of a passion in winter white Maine. He would take to the old roads in the hills back home: in dark night, cutting a swath through trees with the beam of the sleek machine's lamp; hunched and helmeted, burrowing for miles through frosty tunnels of trees.

Visiting the Eastern Uplands

Snow Goer magazine, to which he subscribes, will describe the name Aroostook as a Maliseet word for "shining bright." *The County* is a land wide open of 6400 square miles in forests, fields and freshwater; with a net of trails 1500 miles long, including converted railroad beds where steam locomotives once plied snowy rails. Power lines and old logging roads also provide traces for snow machines. All over Aroostook the modern equivalent of yesteryear's innkeepers host hungry trail-riders in winter.

This is how John Sandberg, writing of "Snowmobiling at the Break of Dawn," promotes the sport in *The County*. Mentioning this Old Mill Marina on Eagle Lake, he tells of its recent history. It was abandoned for fifteen years until a man named Ben Ricciardi decided to put it to use drawing snow riders to this village of 1000. After fifteen years of economic neglect, the wood turning industry gave way to the service sector when he turned the mill into a resort. Many Mainers, more and more, don't turn up their noses at service oriented work: In remote areas it's appreciated. When Aroostook's "shining bright" whiteness, the crystalline form of water falls through the air, they see it as manna from heaven. Snow means money-to-earn. It means skiers and snowmobilers up from Massachusetts, down from Canada. If mill work isn't available, they'll take whatever is sent. This isn't moralizing, its reportage. It's what I've seen since coming to Maine.

The converted mill reminds us of our hamlet's wood mill in Western Maine. All day long I hear that monotone hum of the community's separator. I'm reminded by the sound that we are a working community with a stake in the little mill's survival. Now diminishing, small turning-mills, found in working woods all the way to Canada, provided jobs for local people in these regions. These little communities dotting our state are the health of Maine. But these communities are strongest when their economic supports are diverse, when the life of place is provided for within its own borders—food, building materials, fuel, clothing, schooling. When all this is going on in the village, then the village is whole.

Industry done on the scale of our wood mill is better for us than that of unwieldy and uncaring corporations whose headquarters are in some distant place. As commentator Wendell Berry points out, large corporations cannot care for the community with a genuine affection. The only "community" to which the CEO of a corporation may truly respond is that of the monetary profit of its shareholders. The CEO may not even care for the *well-being* of shareholders. This is why noxious sludge is spread over tracks of what was community forest land, why a community's massive tranquil rivers are turned into toxic sewers, why workers are made to work rotating shifts in fuming factories where the sun doesn't shine. This abuse is authorized for the "lowly" community by absent overseers who have no physical, familial, or emotional stake, here.

A large corporation hunkers powerfully in the community, spreading a gluttonous weight on its earth in concrete, iron and steel. In power transfer stations, winders and conveyors, stacks, great vats; motors screaming. It's a beast of iron, stamping the residue of human and animal communities beneath its maddening malevolent feet. But it is all food for the virtually invisible microbial iron eaters. The scope of true caring is small, mostly manageable. It's the size of a friendship, a family, neighborhood, a community. It matches our own size. We are small.

The marina's restaurant is under consideration for lunch. Its slanted designer wood siding and atrium top, glassy and glittery, is perhaps too much for us. Allen runs in to check on the menu but quickly returns after seeing the foyer and stairway: hanging plants, shimmering chandelier, and a pricey looking elevated view of the lake. Not your average roadkill restaurant.

We drive uphill, away from the shore to . . . the *Village Restaurant and Lounge*. Inside we find that the view behind gauze curtains is of gravel parking lot, a house across the street. The walls are papered in deep charcoal blue, lined with a pattern of tiny pink flowers. The establishment is also a conversion, converted house with traditional living-room-dining-room-kitchen configuration. The kitchen is in back, the darkened bar converted from what was once a household dining room. We sit in the "living room," having our order taken by a young waitress with long dark hair and hazel eyes. Goblets clink as she sets them on the table and pours our water.

"What do people do here for a living?" I ask after the opening courtesies.

"That's just it. There's nothing." She says her grandfather was a storekeeper and now her father rents videos. A recent graduate, in high school she rode an hour to school—each way—on the bus to Fort Kent up the Fish River Road. What would the historic road-builder Gervis (who worked for decades in all weathers with horse and axe to complete the primitive road); what would he think of this?—Fort Kent in an hour. Would he be starstruck? Surprised? Grateful his labor of a lifetime prepared for our ease? Or would he counsel us to buy a strenuous life, tried in some crucible—making spiritual, clothing our nakedness? Maybe go back to the one-room school?

I ask about the Old Mill Marina, which seems too pricey for locals.

"No one can afford it," she says. "It's all gold in there."

The food comes. I devour light turkey sandwiches and tea. Then I get up and cross through the darkened bar to ask for more tea at the kitchen door, where I overhear the French-speaking proprietor. Upon returning to our table and some talk with Allen, I notice for the first time a white corner cabinet behind my chair, French provincial. Striking in the charcoal blue room. I sit down to drink my tea but cannot help looking back over my shoulder at it. Surreptitiously I take stock of the contents, even as we share murmured conversation.

On the top shelf sits a brandy snifter filled with green and lavender potpourri. Lower shelves hold tiny goblets, gold filigree. One set is rimmed in gold, the second has a leaf design, a third is coated in gold. A set of glittering geode bookends; a porcelain loon with chick. My eye drifts to the curtains of the window—fine white gauze with sashes. From curtains to wallpaper and cabinet, everywhere we find that flair, a touch of modest French country styling.

After paying the bill we step outside where I notice a wooden ramp beside the steps. A wheelchair ramp, weathered but in repair, and not, at this writing, required by law. A thoughtful measure. Yet, I'm not thinking of the ramp, but of a modest dwelling converted into an eatery: quietly and beautifully providing a service. I'm thinking, *It's all gold in there.*

Logger Activists

DRIVING SOUTH, DOWN TOWARD Portage. Through Winterville. I'm drowsy from lunch and hot tea at Eagle Lake, but must keep watch for Portage where we turn off to head back to Caribou, which we hardly saw in passing. We pass now through Quimby country. A lake off to the right, glimpsed going downhill. Kendall, in his *Glaciers & Granite*, mentions Portage. Something about the fine line between the big woods and mixed woodland/farmland. This long ridge we've been traversing since leaving Fort Kent is a geographer's stone, divining the boundary between the endless forest and fair farmland.

Once again we are encouraged to think about edges, borders, boundaries. The social and spiritual concept of *bounds*—of humility—is as old as law. It was perhaps refined as the Middle Ages approached into the Renaissance, courtesy in full flower. Since the advent of Western exploration, conquest, and the Industrial Revolution, propriety has all but sunk out of sight, as Westerners especially persist in rejecting personal bounds. And yet courtesy might save the situation, a relationship, a community. A planet.

Descending we see young ragged woods, stretching, reaching away into distance. The big woods appear to be very young—at least from the Aroostook Road. To the West I see another long ridge—"like an Appalachian Ridge," says Allen—but low, covered with trees into the distance. We descend and the view becomes blocked by a virtual wall. At the roadside are thin willowy tamaracks, or larches or hackmatacks as they are variously known. Still green. Soon they will gleam golden beneath somber skies like candles in the cathedral. Then, even though they are conifers, they will shed all their needle-leaves. This trip convinces me of what I've read often enough. There is now no old-growth forest. It's been cut, cut, and cut again. The spindly thickets are the latest generation of the disappeared ancients,

Visiting the Eastern Uplands

descent of the ages, of primeval forest grown out of tundra in the wake of purging glaciers.

Now the wood edges up to our road, distant visions of woods and water pass. We are surrounded by trees in flaming colors, inset with the old-dark-spiny-green of spruce, of fir. A few large diameters can be found—only six or eight inches, sometimes ten. Mostly they are much thinner—two or three inches in diameter. Township 14, range 6, says the sign.

Drowsy, inattentive. . . . We ascend a bit to another mountainous view—blue undulations, boggy land remotely, a lake. The road in this remote place is being restructured a bit, dug up. Here are piles of exploded rock, shale-looking, slate. An oily smell penetrates through closed windows. Gravel here is sharp enough to blow out a tire. Still, the place is Sabbath-abandoned.

On and on driving. On and on. The gravel road. I'm drowsing a little. A bit later, I'm saying with a touch of anxiety, "Think we passed Portage . . . I know I'm supposed to be navigating . . . but I never saw a settlement."

Allen is irritated. "I saw a road, but didn't think it was *the* road. It was only dirt or gravel."

It's been a long drive.

Here, for the first time en route, we're about to quarrel. We have inadvertently passed Portage, passed our crossroads. We've gone all the way down to Ashland.

Portage is past. *Portage,* the word for carry-your-canoe-to-next-water, is a slight path between navigable bodies, humble but essential in the wilderness. But here Portage means loggers at work in the woods, a part of the designated life of Aroostook. In *The County* are a few loggers, a few farmers, a few goods and services, and some towns like Caribou, Fort Kent, Eagle Lake, Madawaska. Workers all make a modest living, carrying them from one week or water to the next.

In the near future, when I'm ready to put this venture on paper, there will be a segment on Maine Public Radio, warning that "logger activists" are headed this way from the Northwest—*The* Northwest—from Washington, Oregon, Idaho. They will be coming, according to reporter Keith Shortall, to fight "well-paid environmentalists."

In Portage no one has seen either yet. In Portage you know what loggers know: "If you don't work in the woods, you don't have a job." The reporter's interpretation is true, whether said in English or French, because

Logger Activists

Portage is on the other side of the geographer's stone. It is beyond the edge, beyond farm and town, and into the woodland.

It seems unlikely that logger activism originated in the woods. I smell a corporation—one with a team of PR and interpersonal consultants. Keith Shortall will report about a video, brought from *The Northwest*, pointing out that a portion of the setting is industrial. It's a motivational video, urging loggers to unite. In this production a logger activist will stand up and attempt to empower other loggers present to fight back should high paid environmentalists strike. He'll pump'em full of words, ask them to hold hands, raise them high, and "repeat after me. . . ." The response will be some lackluster, making it appear that they are not comfortable with this bar-and-chain oil.

I'm acquainted with a very few loggers. Certainly not enough to fill a room. I can't picture any of them holding hands. Or raising arms to repeat after me. The loggers I know are, without exception, humble men. They are largely quiet in company. I was once alone with one in a living room for five minutes before I became aware of his presence. Not only do they work outdoors, early, any weather, they *are* the outdoors. Natural, reminding one of a stray breeze moving through remote bows. I hope to God they stay that way.

We slid right past Portage and landed in Ashland. Carried our canoe to the next water and went on. I hope the logger activists will do likewise. (Environmentalists, too.)

Good Work

ASHLAND. WE ARE SOUTHWEST of Caribou and Presque Isle, looking for a route to lead us. A view opens up. A few fields and woodlands, some houses widely scattered. White houses, light roofs, the sun glancing off. Some are asphalt shingle, dark; some shining metal. A metal roof sheds snow—a must in western and northern Maine. In snow country a roof may be bowed by one season's ponderous weight. Folks without metal roofs must climb up and shovel after each white-fall. Otherwise one could have nine feet overhead by season's end, despite the January thaw. The oldest layers turn to ice underneath, as though hewn granite stacked meters thick on your flimsy house. The old caved-in gambrels along Aroostook roadsides are testament of this.

Besides volcanic looking Mars Hill, there is another anomaly in Aroostook: a vast difference in snowfall amounts between Caribou and Presque Isle, the former only twelve miles north of the latter. Over a thirty-seven year period, from 1951 to 1980, the recorded difference between these two towns was a whopping 27 inches. Readings taken at the two area airports showed that Presque Isle's average annual accumulation was 93 inches, while Caribou's was 120 inches. That's nearly seven-and-a-half compared with ten feet of snow on the roof each year. Like The County itself, each house might have its own mini glacier.

A couple of old white clapboard churches with signboards and steeples. *Ames Hotel*, dining room and lodge. *Taxidermist. Canoes,* rentals. We see private houses with signs out for various services. *Guiding. Crafts and Gifts. Beauty shop. Sun-tanning. Alterations.* It's the same in our part of Western Maine. People know how to eke out their livings: to shovel out from under the weight of winter, keep a barn full of harvest. They work at low-paying jobs, and hang their shingles. *Expeditions. Horseback-riding.*

Good Work

We travel on toward Caribou. The farmlands are back, solidly. We're in the center now, the woodlands left behind. Satellite dishes; few if any houses for sale. CB antennas: The Maine Potato Net comes to mind—a network of ham radio operators who meet on air of an evening in winter.

Washburn. Potato land. Fields rising up on ridges, the long silver warehouses of agribusiness. A mechanical harvester on a distant ridge, silhouetted, motionless against the sky. This eerie motionless version of potato harvests has struck me on this trip. Aroostook fields, in their harvests, do not look the busy swarming fields I thought they would. I'd expected fields full of young bent backs, teenagers out of school for the purpose; squatting over steep rows littered with potatoes, millions of bright speckles on a field of dirt-brown. It's why I mistook piled chunks of limestone for piles of potatoes. Potatoes, I thought, were supposed to be *visible* during a harvest. But that was last decade's version. A decade ago mechanical diggers, not harvesters, unearthed the spuds and youngsters came along and thrust them into baskets.

A supplement in the Caribou and Presque Isle papers this week, *Harvest Heritage*, is full of accounts of former potato pickers. Reprinted from *Echoes, The Northern Maine Journal of Rural Living*, Kathryn Olmstead's article tries to pinpoint how the famous harvest recess got started. Each year Aroostook schooling starts up two weeks before that of Maine's other schools. The kids are in school for a month until harvest recess in mid-September when they go to work, either in the fields or at other jobs, for three weeks. Every year there's a tug-of-war between farmers and school administrators, the latter always threatening to do away with this recess. About 50% of students actually work the harvest, with another 30 doing other work, the remainder doing what they will.

According to the minutes of Caribou School Committee meetings, the recess was implemented in 1948. Prior to this the schedule varied from that of the rest of the state and school began during the first or second week in October and extended to the last week in June. So potatoes have always been harvested by the young. They scooped spuds out of the earth for 12 to 14 hours a day. Today they assist on mechanical harvesters, standing under a canopy tossing rotten potatoes from the conveyor by the hour.

The newspaper supplement gives us a feel for the richness of life during a rugged harvest time. Sunny weather lit by foliage; harsh weather chilled by frost or a cold drenching stream from the sky. Mornings of darkness and teenage aching muscles, piping breakfasts and sleepy wait for a truck ride to the field. Harvests turned ordinary work-at-home mothers into messengers of mercy who stopped by the field with an extra snack or an extra hand among the spud baskets. Kimberly Wright of Presque Isle tells what it felt like. "The damp soil kept my knees cool as I moved forward in my section. My efforts left a telltale pattern in the soil: small trenches where my knees dragged along; footprints back and forth from the rows of potatoes to the barrels, where I'd emptied my basket about four times before filling a barrel. By lunchtime I might have picked 14 barrels."

Besides blesséd well-fed rest at the end of each day, there was a glad reward of trips to town on Saturday night. Everyone congregated. Stores stayed open late to accommodate kids who now had spending money in addition to savings for college, or clothing, or Christmas.

Margaret Kimball of Caribou worked in her folks' store, witnessing the activity and excitement. "There were those who chose to sit in their parked cars, watching people walk by. Back and forth, in and out of the stores, the crowds came and went. Sometimes these motorists stayed parked all evening, entranced by the activity, the laughter, and the chatter of neighbors, friends, and the strangers who came from afar."

In an article called "Helping the Farmer," by Kathryn Olmstead, six seniors from the University of Maine remembered working the harvest. (Quotations used with permission of Ms. Olmstead.)

"Getting up at 4:30 in the morning."

"Going to bed and hearing the tractors."

"And you see the rows . . ."

"And you just close your eyes and your mother's calling you to get up."

"And you get dirty. Holy. . . ."

"My fingernails looked like a werewolf's."

"The feel in your mouth, that grit. . . ."

"Did your back bother you, working on the harvester? Mine did. . . ."

Good Work

"It's kind of sad to see it go; you feel like kids are missing something. They're just like everybody else now, like kids from Portland or Bangor. County kids are special because they've had the experience of hard work, they've been initiated...."

"The whole community comes together."

"You realize that's how farmers are making a living and you have a part in that. You don't want to let them down."

We cross the shallow soil-rich Aroostook River and go into Washburn Village, flanked by houses set back from the road. Many large, sprawling white houses. Again we are reminded of central small-small town Ohio: of Smithville, and Dalton where Amish lived and worked, and Marshallville with its Marshallville Meats. The Baptist Church. The Pentecostal church with sign—*Happy Anniversary, 75 years*. (To everyone a shingle.)

With a population of 318, the town was incorporated in 1861, a few months before Civil War was declared. It was named in honor of Israel Washburn Jr., then governor of Maine, and founder (with others) of the Republican Party. Long wondering if the town was connected to the Washburn family, I discovered this fact on one of the many rewrites of this book—and 25 years after this initial Aroostook journey. Israel was the seventh among the generations Washburn to be so named, but he was called Gabe. He grew up along with the farmstead in Livermore, Maine, and worked with the large Washburn family in its building and cultivation during hard winters and hard times. He donated land for the Universalist Church building very near the gracious Victorian mansion (a connected dwelling) that replaced the family farmstead destroyed by fire. Israel had a hand in harvesting and cider-making, and later he renovated the old orchard with great care. By then it was a labor of love, a careful rebuilding of soils requiring manure and lime plaster with ashes, as prescribed. According to Dr. True of Bethel, writing in 1859, it would have been planted in potatoes to help make the soil porous.

During those times Henry David Thoreau equated cultivated apples with things heavenly, in a metaphor of their fragrance. The fragrance that profit could not completely get its hands on. Though the farmer may handle his apples, he cannot handle the "stream of their evanescent and celestial qualities going to heaven from his cart."

Visiting the Eastern Uplands

Here, at Washburn in Aroostook County, are the modest cool mansions in spacious small town America. Do I need to bring nuance and balance to this piece? To mention that here, as in communities everywhere, we'd find a complex of personal problems? To dispel the glow with grit? But you know all that. For Governor Israel Washburn, this life in The County was conducive to aid or console these personal struggles, whether hidden or revealed to one's neighbors—struggles to which we are born. Before crushing snowfall, this is the place where the crop is largely invisible. The place where kids toss rotten spuds off apparently motionless harvesters, before a mini glacier comes to each household. It's a place devoted to the cultivation and handling of nourishment. It's good work, if you can get it.

The Caribou Loams

WE ARE TRAVELING NORTH east toward Caribou, that Northern Maine town with mystique in its name. Except in wild winter (as I imagine it), it is almost nothing of what its name suggests. The caribou are gone, despite repeated efforts to revive their wild, antler-and-furred presence in Maine. The dusty moth-riddled stuffed heads of this North American reindeer may adorn walls of sporting-goods shops and restaurants, deer and moose may munch at the outskirts of town where a mix of scattered woodland, bog, and cropland prevail, but the caribou are gone. The pervasive presence of humans whose culture was increasingly hostile to nature drove them into the north well over a century ago. The Abenaki, or People of the Dawn, told that the damming of forest-streams (done in order to get the wood out) repelled them. Yet caribou, like the prophets, have left a legacy in their name. On long winter nights, when an arctic breath surges through town, the civilized and cemented environs yet must feel that wildness which the word caribou still invokes.

Caribou, with its shops and services, has elms and maples bordering its rising streets. Like the campus at Presque Isle, it has decorative beauty in limestone. "Lots of Limestone, but no caribou," comments Allen. Here Limestone won't be easily chased off by civilization.

Neat white houses and tree-spangled yards climb Caribou's slopes above the Aroostook River. Perhaps this hill, holding the town in tiers, accounts for the difference in snow amounts between it and Presque Isle, a scant twelve miles to the south. For every 25 foot rise in elevation, there's a corresponding one inch increase in snowfall—one reason why Maine has a progressive increase in overall amounts from its coasts to its northern uplands and western mountains.

Burger King and MacDonald's. There's a sign posted outside the latter's restroom, closed at 7 p.m.: *sorry for the inconvenience*. A sign on the side door of Burger King says the door will be locked at 9 p.m. due to vandalism. *Sorry*.

We land finally in the spacious Caribou Motor Inn (surely an oxymoron?). I'm tense from the long ride in a cramped car. It is work to be attentive, to record observations over long periods. I recline, sprawled on the double bed, slowly absorbing half a beer. Allen flips through the channels of international television. "It's fun," he says. . . . *Zap zap zap*. I'm falling asleep.

Shortly to awaken, groggy. *Zap zap zap*. Allen is still at it. Now he turns off the TV, goes into the hall and down to see the swimming pool. I'm still coming awake.

A floor plan of the Caribou Motor Inn is on a table beside the television. After a bit I get up to look at it. The plan is approximately square with an inner square, containing pool and courtyard lounge, all enclosed within the building. There are four banquet rooms, a second lounge, dining room, weight room, locker rooms, tanning booths, saunas, and about 60 or 70 guest rooms.

I decide to go see Allen seeing the swimming pool. Walk down the hall, turn left past soda machines, stand outside the Court/Pool. Look through glass out over empty tables, octagonal bar in the midst of a vast enclosed court. Blue-white reflections shimmer in twilight. The pool is Olympic, divided from the lounge by a median with potted (plastic?) plants. Allen is nowhere in sight: No one is there. I plaster my face against the glass. At once his face appears opposite, grinning.

He opens the door, I step into the deserted court. The atmosphere in here is moist, faintly chlorine: nothing like conjured *caribou*. It reminds me of Florida without the blinding light. Together we step down and thread through tables to the octagonal bar. Cupped fistfuls of colored straws provide a decorative touch, giving the empty bar a festive feel. The floor plan said that the Court Cafe is closed during summer. Few days remain of calendar summer. One pictures the now silent and strangely damp places as a lively bright haven, bubbling with conversation and laughter—against subzero cold. When the snow is seven feet deep overhead, come down to the Courtyard Cafe and Pool, open 10 a.m. to 9 p.m. (Well, it is Maine after all).

We stroll poolside, along the length of this mysteriously reflective body of water. Its pale lights ripple over ceilings and walls high above. At

The Caribou Loams

its far end is an inner pool, tiled in brown. The kiddie pool? A touch of my forefinger says it's a hot tub.

Later we find stairs leading down from the pool to a lower level where locker rooms, sauna, tanning beds and Nautilus equipment stand idle. No one is about. Here walls and concrete floor are all carpeted. I stick my head into the weight room, flip on the light and eye the machines. One two three . . . I count 15 plus a computerized exercycle and a rowing machine. Allen brushes past, swings a leg over the cycle and begins pumping. Figures for mileage and wattage appear on the display. He pumps harder, faster, the numbers mounting. Finally he yields to my ridicule and dismounts. We exit laughing, poking fun, careful to shut off the light.

Back upstairs, I hear splashing. A lone swimmer is doing laps in the pool of the Caribou Motor Inn.

Allen and I took our evening meal at *Green Acres Restaurant*, just down the open road from the Caribou Motor Inn. This meal was delicate and delicious, the salad bar varied, filled with multiplicity, broccoli, and secrets well-kept but intriguing to the palate. The roll was light, tender, topped with fresh farm butter. Angel hair pasta—lighter still, wonderfully seasoned, delicately evocative Italian. Fine coffee; steak, baked potato. Exquisite desserts regretfully declined. *Full.*

Peeking between slats in the blind, glancing out the window over salad, I was surprised to see real green acres behind the establishment. And beyond . . . one of the rolling ridges of Aroostook, low beneath the vast mellow sky. The scene graded from ripe field to woods crowning the ridge. Sun lighted our view with gold. It was out of sight and sinking somewhere behind as the full earth spun.

I peeked out from time to time as the meal progressed. Twilight was rising through atmosphere. The moon, at first a wan disc of silver, also rose. Towers began glowing on the distant ridge. Radio towers, tall as mountains, slender as thread above dimming green hills and autumnal colors. These hills and colors faded along with the light. The vast blue faded, then darkened. High radio towers began winking—vertically placed gems upon the throat of night. Reminiscent of the tail-lights we had followed to enter this land but two nights before. The moon rose, a shining coin.

We wanted to ask the Base Closure and Realignment Commission: Is this "quality of life"? We wanted to know, I over my baked potato, Allen over his delicate saucy pasta. Is this what is meant? If abundance of woods fields lakes streams; if eagles and moose and coyote and deer . . . if these are not meant . . . then, are swimming pools saunas hot-tubs lounges exercise horseback-riding snow machines golf courses . . . are these the necessary components of quality life? Or do we seek something more? Is there more? Check under the table.

It was dark, but I wanted to find the limestone bedding mentioned in Kendall. We drove back and forth on the highway, looking for landmarks. There. Just down the drive from the rest area. A dark road cut, marbled with faintly gleaming white. Allen braked and turned off the engine. I opened the door, flashlight in hand. Straddling the gully I reached out and broke off a piece of sedimentary rock, of limestone, looked at it in the yellow beam.

A coating of white upon gritty brown reminded me of thin white glazing on a cake: calcite deposits—calcium carbonate effervescent through fissures and solidified in veins. I split the rock apart, brittle along its cleavages, wet in my hand.

I held Aroostook County in my fingers. This was the weathered rock, eroding towards soil—the fertile Caribou loams, producer of potatoes and broccoli and buckwheat and other. When we eat potatoes we eat minerals transmuted from rock. Such rock is the bone-building material of the world. It provides the framework or structure whereby we stand. It's crushed, dismantled, dissolved and finally absorbed by rootlets. Detritus feeds us, quickens these bodies, this hand holding a sample of Aroostook.

Limestone, thou art bread of life, laid down of sediments: the shell and carapace, broken houses of sea creatures eventually crushed by weight of the sea. Limestone in the lowest (under-ocean abyssal plains). Limestone in the highest (roof of the world, Everest). You, generous giver, are wounded to particles, savaged by elements and fed to us as broccoli. There may be no place on this planet that you have not been. And always you leave behind food.

Food of geological ages, of moldering millennia: your name being Limestone, faithful and true. The stone which the builders of bases rejected.

"So It's Not Home"

WE AWAKEN TO A day clouded over, gray and chill. Allen will meet me out front with the car. I stroll through hallways to the lobby of the Caribou Motor Inn and return our key. I pick up a copy of the *Aroostook Republican and News*, "serving Aroostook for 111 years." Dated last Wednesday, September 18, 1991. I scanned newspaper racks all over The County but haven't found a single daily. Not unusual, perhaps, for Maine.

I plunk down fifty cents for this paper because of its headlines. "Loring reuse effort slated for start. . . ." And, "Air Force continues promise to clean up base in three years." This refers to the estimated $400 million cost of cleaning up base-generated toxic dump sites. The list of toxins includes "PCBs, heavy metals and low-level nuclear waste," and "18 sites which contain fuel products . . . some petroleum is seeping into groundwater. . . ." Good waters which saturate precious Caribou loams, now mingled with contaminants. Contributors to quality of life. It shows far better than a vote what an unwieldy federal bureaucratic government thinks of life in Limestone, Maine.

I fold the paper under my arm, push open the door. Passing through I see a small sticker on the glass above the handle. In green, white, and blue, it shows the contour of the northern portion of Maine formed in part by the St. John. An outline of a lonely mountain, its words say *Aroostook, the Crown of Maine*.

We top off our visit of Caribou with a stop for breakfast at a small restaurant called *A Little Bit of Home*. The placemats on the table before us were printed by a company in Bangor but, looking carefully at fine print in a corner, I see that it is a copyrighted product of Springfield, Ohio. The scene is of green woodland with small spruce and large pines, rocks, creepers,

Visiting the Eastern Uplands

blackberry bushes, ferns, mushrooms, pink thistles. It's everything I've been writing about in *Visiting the Eastern Uplands*.

Here bees buzz about a pine full of honey from their prodigious efforts. The big American black bear stands, ripping bark and dead cambium to get at that honey. Two of her cubs noodle around on the ground in front of her. One climbs a fungus-ridden stump, one eats an unripe blackberry, while another noses a butterfly off the thistle (about to get a nose full of spines).

But the scene *was* in fact once typical of Ohio, where forests were so dense that a pioneer could scarcely see through the gloom. The woods there, as here in Aroostook, are now borders. Or there are occasional clusters about houses. Both this portion of *The County* and of Ohio had their trees downed, with massive stumps pulled to make way for crops. Now, apart from Metropolitan Ohio, there remains to these two places both farmland and woodlots upon the rolling green of the nourishing land.

Breakfast is served by a speedy plump woman with teased and smoothed-over blond hair. She wears red-framed glasses. She buzzes around—like one of the bees depicted on the placemats—dispensing coffee, hot platefuls of food. Her every query is punctuated with the word *dear*. She darts toward us: "Is everything OK, dear?" She buzzes away. She buzzes back. "More coffee, dear?" She is solicitous, generous. Yet I sometimes wish someone would take a swipe at her.

She epitomizes the homeyness of this restaurant, whose knickknacks and bric-a-brac and sayings on the walls suggest the home-gone-to-seed experienced by the post-adolescent. I don't feel relaxed enough here to think of it as *A Little Bit of Home*. It's like the embroidered saying hanging on the wall there: "So it's not home—adjust!"

One last swing through the commercial center of Caribou—for postcards of Aroostook. I sit in the car writing messages and addresses on the back of typical scenes. A card for JD in Portland . . . a card for Seth out west . . . and one for Ohio.

One scene is not typical: it's an aerial shot of Caribou. Very green, leafy, dissected with gray lines—lines of streets—and dotted with minute boxy shapes. A beautiful small town, curving over a hill with a river border.

I get out, walk across the street, go into the old brick post office and wait my turn in line for stamps. Ahead of me, three dark men are speaking Spanish. They buy money orders and address envelopes at one of the counters. Migrant farmworkers, sending the bounty of their labor here to some Spanish-speaking home. Laborers for the harvest, then, are not all homegrown in this northern County.

As with many farm states across the nation, Ohio, too, is host to migrant laborers. *Ohio* magazine's "The Man Who Wouldn't Lie Down."—MacArthur Fellowship award winner Baldemar Velasquez who founded the Farm Labor Organizing Committee, FLOC, struggled for years in Ohio to achieve things most take as granted in the workplace: things such as hourly wages as opposed to piecework. These humble people (many of whom are second and third-generation Americans) have subsidized bodies for the rest of us with their own bodies. These are the Americans who do our stoop work at tiny wages in order to provide us with tomato sauce, canned soup, relishes, fruit cocktail—in short, any canned, frozen or fresh food we gulp or savor each day of our lives. Whenever I open a can or dump frozen vegetables into boiling water, I prepare foods whose cost is much lower than it would be if I paid its true worth.

Often migrant workers are not alone when they go into fields to labor for food. With no other place to be, their children go with them. The Associated Press will write next year that about 300 children each year, all migrants, are killed in accidents in fields and camps, with no statistics on those injured.

Migrants are far from home when they labor for our nurture, working in communities where they are often despised. Home folks don't treat them that way. They send wages home, away from their working communities, where their heroism is recognized by loved ones and friends.

If migrant workers may be seen as analogous to soil, its type is Caribou loam: an upright soil full of nurture for those who live by its generosity, workability, bounty. We can acknowledge our debt to it with gratitude. Or—unthinking—we walk on it, little realizing we walk over a body yielded up for our care.

Mars Hill

Going south, the clouds of route 1 are parting in gaps of blue, and layered in levels—torn and drifting at various speeds. Receiving impressions of deep deep sky, vast high halls of heaven, we creep southward, so small beneath, as sunlight alternates with shadow on the windshield of our car.

Allen and I have been talking about perspective and perception as we travel down toward Houlton. He says that returning over the same ground reinforces what we've seen along the way. Yet our face is now set in the opposing direction, yielding a different point of view . . . and an altered perception, an understanding more complex and mature. He comments on the very different appearance of Mars Hill. On the drive north he had seen the lone mountainous cone-shape, an anomaly in this rolling land of Aroostook. But because he was at the wheel he missed the elongation of the ridge behind, which I in my leisure was able to turn and see. Approaching now from the north, he witnesses this ridge and length, this supine body of Mars Hill.

It was cold spring when I began the book before this one in which I desired this visit; a day fierce as winter. We were hiking through snow up the steep side of the ski mountain, thinking about layoffs, bills, family difficulties. Thinking about Hawthorne and progress and the art of the turn. Now I can glance up the side of Mars Hill and see green ski trails, the Big Rock Ski Area. A small skiway, catering to locals. Lost Valley, in Western Maine understands and has capitalized on this local and family niche. At first owner Fern Pontbriand was disappointed when he saw how small the ski mountain was. But Pontbriand was encouraged to learn that most skiers are beginners or intermediates, and that businesses concentrating on families had fallen off 30% nationwide. Those businesses making it did so on personal interest, strong desire. They're out there taking the economic turns as smoothly as they can, hoping the judges take notice. It's the same with raising a family. You're young, in the midst of life, you have a family. Disillusionment sets in, the whole thing begins to look like an anomaly, this family-raising in the fair imagined plain of your life. You turn, it lengthens, stretches out, claims the whole of your attention. And judges are watching.

Later, on my way back northward through this territory, grandparenthood approaches. I'll be older, seeing it all over again at leisure, from a different perspective. It's then we realize that those judges watching us are ourselves, expressing commentary on the text of our lives. We are the judges who can't help but gauge the performance in our execution of life's turns. It looks different because we've been changed by our experience.

The name and classical shape of Mars Hill prompt mythical stirrings, thoughts of imaginative viewpoints: ways of seeing that artists and poets share. They sort through knowledge, insight, experience; arranging these for presentation on canvas, film, or the page. Mountains, Trees, Thrushes and Thistles are what each is for that reason alone. Yet in addition they embody expressions of principle, of Divine Mind. Mind that is immeasurably stronger and surer than humans' own. In response to these expressions, the artist's canvas or page or sounding in air should trigger a like response in viewer, reader or listener. One no doubt slightly different from that intended. The difference is the function of metaphor (as opposed to a "purposed domination" of a reader's mind in allegory, as Tolkien has said).

Even so, the writer, painter or musician controls to a large extent the viewpoint or creative vision presented. This is the operation of imagination. As with any responsibility it should be done with care. One should care for the Viewer, Reader, or Listener being granted, or subjected to, the vision. These works will furnish a mind. I tinker with words that I might furnish and nourish human mind. (Especially my own.) These words have become the meditations of the reader while in the act of reading. Fill my meager mind with mountains, adorn it with trees waving in the wind. Let the two-throated song of a wood thrush sound through it. The artist of whatever medium fills up the soul of those who generously open themselves up to the expression. In the book before this one I wrote of a desktop full of mushrooms, some of which might be food for us, some of which poison.

While traversing southward, we take into account the changing aspect of Mars Hill. Our route aims straight for its massive flank. Now our road veers and we travel alongside the supine giant. Here its shape reminds me of Streakéd Mountain in Western Maine, my geographer's stone, metaphoric guide. But, where Streakéd Mountain is streaked with rock and crowned with a radio tower, Mars Hill is streaked with broad ski trails, green in surrounding autumnal foliage. It has a communications tower up there as well. What is it we communicate from the mythic summit with this ranging artistry? Are there narrow narcissistic ruminations? Now may be time for artists (angry, sorrowful) to roughly shove self-pity aside and raise a lament for creation (á la Julian Lennon, Bruce Cockburn, the late Marvin Gaye. "*Mercy, Mercy Me.*")

The sky above is closing up, shutting high halls behind thick curtains, veils of moving gray. On a ridge top south of Bridgewater I look back to see the lone cone of Mars Hill, silent and gray. Imposing and present in its own land. An anomaly once more.

Roadside potatoes for sale on the long road. Self-service at a new particle-board stand, olive green. Two dollars for 10 lbs.. Pulling off in gravel and dust, Allen has a few phrases for the 18-wheeler riding our bumper. I jump out, dollars in hand and grab for a bag. My money goes into a can already boasting the sale of several.

In the car again I see that the thick paper bag is damp and earthy. The potatoes inside are still dirty with Caribou loam. We pass another stand, not as new, with sign: 10 lbs. for a dollar and a quarter. The past one hundred yards have cost us seventy-five cents.

Around the turn of the 20th century, and into its first decades, Maine was building its reputation in potatoes. The railroad had done its deed in bringing the Aroostook spud to the world. Between World War I and the 1950s The County made Maine king of the tubers, especially of seed potatoes. Then, according to geographer Eldred Rolfe, they got sloppy. Their laurels had turned into couches. They got a reputation for selling seed potatoes as table potatoes; spuds were sold from the field in irregular sizes and put in bags "half full of dirt." Other potato states were gaining every season, producing their own seed crop to boot. The great Northwestern states of Washington, Oregon, Idaho began growing the more popular russets for the french-fry market, gaining the competitive edge. Then dietary habits changed; demand went down before healthy alternatives.

But gradually Maine growers began waking up, offering a better crop and putting zest into marketing. Now potatoes sold wholesale are clean and in many cases of superior grade. The french-fry industry has been cracked and processing occurs in *The County*. With help from the University of

Mars Hill

Maine Agricultural Center, new things are being tried, like the five-year program for testing a strain resistant to fungus.

Looking back over the ground beneath Mars Hill, I guess farmers discovered that success is an anomaly. It needed a body of attentiveness, discipline, and plain hard work to sustain it. They had to go back for insight into the problem, for true entrepreneurial values—in order that their crop might endure. Maybe they've rediscovered that the eater of potatoes is the reason for growing them.

Houlton, and the sun comes through. Rifting clouds, layers of cloud. A quick stop at UM Cooperative Extension for a booklet called *Nutritive Value of Foods*. I clatter down the basement steps of the courthouse, looking for the office and knock on the door to enter. A young woman rifles through shelves for me, finds the booklet and accepts my spare change.

Now I'm out in the basement hallway, glancing over racks full of pamphlets with information on how to do anything: clean a chimney, feed a family, build a bungalow. Is there one for catching water from dry air? Some are scientific and broadening. Here's one I might be able to use: *The Gulf of Maine: Sustaining Our Common Heritage*.

I've lived in the Western Mountains and visited the Eastern Uplands. What's next? Your guess is good.

Prose and Dreams

We pass through Houlton on the old Military Road, flying past the Elm Tree Diner. It's a cloudy afternoon, a sky full of swirls. We're headed for Bangor, but on a back route. Two-A is not what I would call a fast route to somewhere, though once it was the only road connecting Aroostook County with the rest of Maine. It is narrow and desolate, now a lumpy old asphalt road that might at times teem with logging trucks, pulp loaders—but we encounter few. In fact, there seems little of anything but trees along this stretch. Forty miles or about 60 km of scraggly wilderness, if the word wilderness applies. The purist would say this is no wilderness. But, as I look out past the asphalt, using the map on my lap for reference, I realize that there is nothing in any direction but cutover woods and brush. Only creatures living in shelter made without hands would be found here.

    I see ravaged colors of autumn, the short tamaracks and other conifers—brush associated with slowly maturing clearcuts. As we travel on and on, the trance of an almost unchanging scene slips upon me. I half-notice woods snuggling up to the roadside, gaining height. Flaming fall trees overtop us humans . . . yet these are no towering trees. Towering trees make for deep cavernous woods. They block out sky, darken all the land. These scraggly things merely point to the sky.

    Yes, I am sleepy and heavy with travel . . . but I attend somewhat. Just enough to recognize a peculiar cloudy lightness beyond the bright changing trees. This, says Allen driving at my side, must be the result of recent legislation restricting cuts of stands along roadsides and streambeds. The chainsaw may no longer approach so close. Yet policy, while protecting against some erosion, gives the false impression of forests extant. But beyond these colorful living walls are recent cuts which have taken whole forests en masse.

The Micmacs and Maliseet who live in Lands of Good Water had plenty of imagination, enough to see mind expressed all around them. Enough to tell stories of wisdom, clarity, breath and spirit. But they lacked the limitless imagination necessary to fall whole forests. Their sense of reality was greater than that. The industrialized imagination thinks that because it can conceive of beginning a thing it can control the thing begun. The Micmacs and Maliseet knew better. Native American myths show us that they did.

When we crest some rare ridge I nudge myself awake enough to look around and, still. . . . Still I see the Maine papermaking forest. Forest cutover, reduced to raw material, strewn through desolate land. One could get lost here, a bare quarter-mile from the road. One could be lost and never heard from again, so empty of humanity and human habitation is this place. To the east lies ten miles of puckerbrush, US route 1 and provincial Canada; to the west hunkers 900 km of ruined wilderness.

When I walk in woods or climb a mountain, I don't mind hearing the saw. It means someone is working outdoors, earning a living for a family. Woods aren't meant for me alone—a scribbler who finds them ravishing and mindful. Allen works in a paper mill. We too make a living from them. That this land is devoted to woodland and woods economy makes me more glad that I can say. Pure corporate ownership, at this point, is preferable to development.

What I care about is that a forest be a forest. That it be loved. It should be high and deep and varying in age. Why can't it be harvested selectively, wisely and well? Shouldn't a forest look and feel like a forest, heal like one, mingling with sky where it exchanges breath in a divinely wrought mutual dependency? Beyond these blazing trees are blasted woodlands, strewn with leavings of looters—the owners themselves have plundered their own lands, leaving an empty shambles.

And yet, my heart could croon a low sad song over the fringed beauty left behind. For it is desolate and still—though yet creeping with wildlife adapted to clearcuts and their aftermath. And the desolation prods and calls to me. I've never ridden such a road, such a lonely forsaken highway. The land "beyond the beauty strip" is shot with bogs, heaped with brush, drifting with the emptiness of fallen stewardship—like wreaths of cloud, these great ghosts above us which even now persist.

Once, nestled in bed, I dreamed of living beneath a forest deep and high with trees. The way trees were meant to grow. I lived in a lodge made of deadfall (made without hands, I suppose). Filled with joy, and running out in vast exhilaration, I plunged my face in new snow. And winter had no weight at all. Winter, it seemed, was solid joy. In returning to my lodge again I took hold of living branches. Their feel in my grip astonished me. Life so stirring fresh it woke me. And I lay in bed, my hands remembering the feel of it.

All day afterward I lay my hands on things, trying to feel that life again. I grasped the wood door frame, ran fingers along knotty pine paneling. But life was gone. Not there. No longer in my feeble fingers, in my palms. Life was in a place where I can only go in prose (halfway), and in dreams.

We travel on and on. On and on. This is the route leading to a route that will take us home. I began writing the book before this one a-year-and-the-half ago with an entry on our hunger and trouble. Today we've come down from eastern uplands, where food is bountiful, its making-land ripe and full. The backseat is piled with apples, potatoes, newspapers, postcards, books, research and photocopies, cassette tapes and more. A veritable harvest of words. In my head are clustered memories of a place perhaps richer than I may see again.

We are coming down out of the Uplands, on a peculiarly forsaken road. Winter is coming. But we don't come down empty. God has filled His barns. Tonight our souls may be required of us.

Uplands Interlude

JUST FINISHED THE SO-CALLED final edit of *Visiting the Eastern Uplands*, first written nearly three decades ago, scarcely looked at since the last of many "final edits," long ago. And I'm discouraged and dissatisfied. I did not achieve worthwhile memoir after leaving the Western Mountains, after launching myself (and spouse!) toward my creative longing. I had desired to visit Aroostook and penetrate its mystique, but could only afford a flying pass-through, spending most of that journey on the road, site-seeing. There may be too much at secondhand here. And too much tonal flame and brimstone. Mine was a younger soul by almost two decades. I could chase after the metaphor but not so craftily compress depth into that two or three days' ride—the surfing of a stranger across the plain of cropland and comment. I can in no way do justice to the dear strange-yet-familiar further County of desire.

So I have begun again, in hopes of better telling, by looking at and including the gift I was given—of seeing The County again—17 years after the first rather facile sighting and report. My hope, what I'm trying to do, is redeem my earlier look and telling, especially trying to get the self-righteous tone out of what follows, reflecting (in so doing), 17 years worth of understanding. I may repudiate the tone but not the judgments of the first part. Its thoughts and metaphors were, and maybe still are, common to me. The first part of this book remains what it was. I don't change it, or pretend the tonality expressed did not happen. There it is, as we have read. At the same time, what comes next may be looser, not as formal. Read now for what came in maturity. What came after we moved over the ridge into the valley behind my Swan's Ledge lookout. See Maine Metaphor's previous books. I'm hoping for better things in the ongoing. Just as I hope for better things beyond this pilgrim's current travels in time and place.

Visiting the Eastern Uplands

Into the Personal Journal, Book Notes, Road Notes

Alone in the Western Mountains

Slept on the porch, so must cope with the mold spore headache.

Riding bikes from home—stifling. Meal preparations. Allen splits kindling, push-mows the yard about the garden. Military jets fly low overhead, practicing. Steaks to grill with mushrooms, hard-necked garlic from Carter's farm. Hard-boiled eggs for salad, lunch. Allen goes off to Deb's hairdressing shop to get some handmade soap. She's an *artiste*, puts all kinds of good stuff in those soaps.

Sinuses still throbbing.

Garden looks good but seems unproductive at the moment. Thought I saw a ripening cherry tomato. Must go down and get it before something else does. Then fix sandwiches. Will soon be too hot to sit out here.

The next day. Sitting on the porch at the Mouse and Bean with Allen before he leaves from here in the mill's pickup truck. Listening to 1940s radio, news, and music, "living" history.

Lonesome, immediately, on his leaving for Frostburg, Maryland.

And the next day. Feel empty.

It got better on beginning work. And Seth called. He invited me over for a day. Said his fowl flew the coop the day before. The guinea fowl went exploring and did not come back.

—Making a mess trying to write in Serendipity Cafe. He called again, began to say the birds were back, just now coming down his drive! I could hear them over the phone sounding jubilant. They found *home* again. Amazingly all were there, after two days and nights wandering in woods. He had reconciled himself to having quail only (next season). He learns anew what a pain live responsibilities can be. I like my loved ones' learning. But the quail will rejoice him. Sandwich gone—got to leave—the sun and seven miles to go . . . unless . . . the Rabbit Road, maybe?

Make it to the Cinnamon Stick, resting from the woodsy streamy swampy territory, the heat, humidity. Bugs. Joyce's smile passing by in the midst of Sunday-serving is especially friendly and healing. Iced coffee. The bugs out there are mainly deer flies—I call them hair flies—and mosquitoes. All told, did about—what?—twelve miles of beauty in torment to avoid seven miles on the sweltering highway with pulp trucks, semis, etc.? Bugs swarming, biting so much. They seem the very symbol of travailing mental

Uplands Interlude

pricks and ticks, thorns—coming at us like biting flies. One can come indoors to escape the latter, not so the former . . . but there are things one *can* do for mental or emotional relief. Pray, get mentally busy, do something for someone. These are not surefire but far better than nothing. And in this case, what is *nothing*? To cultivate them? Say, "Here bugs, bugs. Come get your dinner? Bring your bro's and sisters'?"

—Okay another thing: laughter!

Following the Anne Morrow Lindbergh suggestion for Allen's absence this week, I refuse the incessant tidying and chores, except for the essential meal-getting, etc. . . . Will leave things lie.

Allen is gone. I will write, read *more*, bike, look, think more—if it's *real* thinking, not the trivia passing for thought. I will—turn into a veritable *man* of the 1950s and '60s as regards domestic and personal habits. (Or maybe this is a fable. It was not so of my dad.)

We will exchange e-mails of an evening, packets of them. He in Milford on his way to Luke.

On the porch after showering now, at the white tile table. Bit of a breeze.

To work on stuff . . . if I don't laze out.

Simple ways of doing things: leave clean dishes in the washer and folded laundry in the basket until needed. Or don't fold laundry! Rinse and use a dirty dish, especially if its contents were innocuous. Having stowed it in the fridge, use a pot again before washing. Do not make the bed. Beds air better, too. Aside: pick ticks off with tweezers when you find them on you. Use as many paper napkins as needed, wear less clothes. Use clothes again before washing.

Seth gives me a tour of the guinea fowl coop, cheap fencing made of horizontal saplings with spikes nailed to trees. The garden, an experiment in piled bedding, going good. Pumpkins amazing. The fowl look a bit like small perfectly black-and-white speckled turkeys, but haughty. Originating in Africa, domesticated, seed and insect eaters. Ground-nesting like what Mainers call partridge—grouse. The fowl may be related to vultures and mate for life. He doesn't seem to like them. I think I smell guinea fowl supper down the road before the quail get here.

Expect to hear from Allen soon. It is now 7:14 p.m.. Time to put this away. A big journal day and not nearly all told.

Second "Flight" to the Eastern Uplands

Now I'm sitting in a park nearly three hours and two hundred miles away. Building a pile of rough notes. By the Penobscot River not far from the Medway confluence with the West Branch. I wrote about that confluence in the first Maine Metaphor book, and something about Mount Katahdin. We have here the great green Aroostook light I remember though I am yet in Penobscot County. I wrote we, but it's just me adventuring . . . some . . . while Allen the paper mill *thermographer* does a stint in Luke, Maryland.

Here are families and couples swimming and picnicking. It's been a very hot day as Maine goes. I saw 93° on a bank sign going through Bangor. Very long drive and not sure why I've come.

Change of place? Refreshment? Set some personal rumination in the regular journal? The one I planned to bring but ended up with this scatter-shot travel journal and notes instead. I hope I can do the travel part justice. The main reason why, however, is the Muse emboldening me. I think I came at His suggestion. It was all settled earlier today on the back deck over coffee . . . in the space of about two minutes, or maybe it was two seconds. The thought was just there, *and it was good*. The ordinary run of work did not seem the thing. Even the writing of fan fiction, *Isildur's Bane*.

I planned—tent camping . . . then realizing that I could get a small inflatable mattress down the road from home cinched it. This would spare accommodation money, but really I wanted to tent camp and needed to be comfortable—. However tonight I am to stay at Gateway Inn on 157 in Medway.

In this park, voices of children float up to me from the river water, a swift flow . . . must be a refreshing swim? I will have to go for a wade. Two young men in dark T's and baggy shorts fish from a dock in the green-reflecting moving water. Shore a couple hundred feet opposite is green from bank to treetop wall, the length of river visible to me. The East Banch River of the Penobscot. In the mythology of Maine at the confluence with the West you would find *Norumbega*. The land of tall dark trees and waters was here, and the legend (a traveler's tale) incorporated among some maps made in Europe (of a land with golden cities), while Maine had scarcely name, borders or identity such as we now find in this once dark corner of the continent.

Would it be fun to write *Norumbega* fan fiction? Look this stuff up again and find . . . Champlain trying to verify the fabled location nearly 80

Uplands Interlude

years after its first mention by a Fench explorer, *Allefonsce*—a land full of "clever inhabitants," with a rich city at the confluence of two rivers.

Dipping feet—my chronically injured foot—in the Penobscot after driving all day—nice. The foot permanently injured in the ice storm ten years ago. So refreshing. Silty covering on the underwater rocks. Some grasses and water weeds there.

Kids and teens get up an impromptu volleyball game. There is a net. A man dressed in green on a green bike, shoulder-length light hair. He roots in the trash cans. The bike has two rear wheel baskets. Can't tell if he got anything. I do not like to show much interest. His head shakes spasmodically when our eyes meet. I wonder about this. The light was golden, is getting greener, as the sun sinks. But after I leave here, everything will be a cool gray.

A couple young women kayakers swifting past, pastel paddles turning. Their kayaks are pastel, too. A jet ski froths along the opposite shore, a font of silver lifting him along. The breeze drops down to us here on these green shores. What could be more fabled than this? It is God's blessing. God enlivens all.

This is nice. I'm surprised and pleased. It is the unexpected flight to the eastern uplands.

Should look for historic forts or museums or something on this trip. The libraries, of course. And bookstores. Maybe in Houlton tomorrow, a.m.. A second cup of coffee there. Glad I did not camp tonight. The ground was not appealing, very woods-dark, hot and buggy in that campground. The proffered site isolated and far from the washroom. There were too many crammed-together big campers in the front part, but with trees, less insects buzzing, and crowds of folk moving together, a variety of moods and movements—some kids popping like corn in the playground.

But this riverside public and free park is alive too, spacious-gracious and happy-like. Am glad I did not "make" myself do the other sleep. I did feel nervous on the approach to the counter inside the camp store, but unwisely disregarded the inner unhappy movement . . . thinking somehow . . .? I don't know . . . the alternative too relieving? Why don't we follow on these kindly impulses, or why hang back when they are spiritually offered? I tried to override the nervous feeling, as being shyness about meeting her and needing to overcome it, when perhaps it was my spirit warning me away. I did think maybe this self-kindness of foregoing was too extravagant.

Visiting the Eastern Uplands

The room ended up costing twice as much . . . for about six times better. Want to learn kindness and be kind to others, especially, and maybe even to myself. I am almost 60. But, through the nerves, I thought I *had* to do that campground.—oh no, more personal monitoring.

Place is empty of young. Darkening but still with faint glowing of dusk. Now older folks sit on a pontoon boat fishing in the midst of the East Branch River. Anchored and gracious. The water a deep green except where light falls upon its surface.

The Gateway Inn looked good, but I wonder will there be sleep? A wish to pitch that tent here on this grass!

A Wheel within the Wheel of Making

As I sat on the deck in the Western Mountains yesterday I thought briefly of visiting the coast. Aroostook is a surprise. Allen will wonder.

Not a bad night at the Gateway where I write now in the Common Room over coffee with instant creamer, and juice (orange) and milk. Two workers (women) sit in the great room, talking. I might ease drop (eavesdrop) but don't (this time). I plan the day or visualize . . . and how will it actually turn out? How will Faith move the subatomic particles and vast empty spaces in "my" vicinity? Have I plans and prayers? And how much pull have these astride great gravity's whereabouts?

I've been reading "The Mountains of Pi" (from the literary nonfiction book), by Richard Preston. About the Chudnovsky Brothers. They were calculating digits of pi, and they said to Preston, "you mustn't," meaning, don't write about us: *We aren't interesting.* Aroostook—even some Mainers have kidded—write about that? Where's the interest? But these Chudnovsky protests made Preston think he was really onto something. To these brothers numbers were perfection, beautiful, more complex, and more actual than any physical matter. It reminds me about what the fine-artist Nancy Jacob said of the Angel they saw in Pennsylvania. Paraphrasing to the best of my recollection: "It was inhuman, more like a mathematical formula." And this also brings to mind the weird or frightening concentric circular beings of CS Lewis' narrative in *Perelandra*. And of Ezekiel's wheel within the wheel. I always thought of pi—how many times a circle's diameter will fit around its periphery—as 3.14. But in reality the approximation is "unfathomable. No apparent pattern is expressed for the intellect as its expansion proceeds . . . forever. Even though this phenomenon comes from precision

Uplands Interlude

of numbers, it seems to me evidence for God's irrational aspect (if aspect is the word—maybe a *quality* (one of multitudes) is a better word). Divinely irrational, concomitant with divine rationality.

Gregory Chudnovsky reminds me of Johannes Kepler in the method of his working. Kepler said he recorded all of his mistakes as would a New World Explorer. Gregory's apartment is dense with works, papers; his theories and discoveries scattered throughout, mixed in with a lot of research and some odd bits like Kipling. And this Chudnovsky may be onto something: it wasn't until Newton that Kepler's laws of planetary motions were unearthed from the ponderous mass of his scriptural circuitry, full also of blind alleys (to thoroughly mix the metaphor). The ratio of the circumference to the diameter cannot contain God. This is why many scientists are able to believe in God—because they know pi is, and cannot be found (here paraphrasing Preston on pi). Chudnovsky has said mathematicians claim the (eventually) disclosed triviality of mathematical findings—given that small findings tend to take an inordinate amount of time and work to achieve.

Since pi stands for periphery in English, it conjures peripheral vision, with which things are glimpsed indirectly. And some things are invisible except to this side vision. Some stars are invisible to direct sight, which registers colors, but some starlight is gathered in the eye's corners instead. Turn to focus on it and that star—has vanished. This has always fascinated me and I have fictionalized it. And it is elsewhere in *Maine Metaphor*.

But still, Preston says, the brothers aren't sure what God is trying to say by this.

I'm thinking... maybe?—"Boys, *I am not trivial.*"?

The plan: Pack. Take I-95 to Houlton, hope for coffee, park, bookstore—in that order? Laze around, look at the day? Then drive on that long loping Route 1 to Presque Isle and find a campground, set up the tent. The plan or the hope to bike ride is now forlorn. I will not be able to bike in this day's heat. The only chance is early a.m. and evening. The pen drives across the page....

Guess one of these workers is the Gateway domestic. The other is the woman at the desk last night—the owner? Not too friendly, typically Mainer toward strangers? Especially those who are socially inept, (seemingly) rude, or possessed of charmless personalities? Think I'll step outside with the coffee.

Visiting the Eastern Uplands

Saw a farm wagon built maybe 100–125 years ago. After a bit of survey—could picture a man making it. Could. Iron-bound wooden spoke wheels, roughhewn wooden bed. Can't picture a man working on most stuff I see today, not like these wagon-wrights worked. One sees hefting musculature, his caring, or complete affinity and fidelity to what he was making in those days. The wagon was parked on slate paving stones, sharp flat rocks, scattered but purposeful. Back inside the Gateway to pay my bill. And when I mention the wagon and the way it was pieced together—that's when the woman shows friendliness. Admit. It was a calculation of mine.

What Am I Doing in Aroostook?

Sitting in scenic view turnout—for scenic Mt. Katahdin—which is blocked by trees. I'm in the car. A couple motorcyclists, taking the view—cameras, cigarettes, motorcycle jackets. I think about You making everything. Keeping track of everything and am a bit worried, astonished. How—!? All the mechanism, and everything, even the social, has its mechanism and its subdivided mechanisms. Go beyond the surface, find another surface, *ad infinitum.*

They leave and I climb out to see the Greatest Mountain. It looks old and scarred and filled brim up with deep heartache above the water spread green and blue below me. People have been lost there, people have died. It is like the earth. And people have been saved after great hardship, trouble, madness (delirium).

It is morning. I get into the backhatch after hard-boiled eggs, half a peach. Stand out there eating these, "viewing." Katahdin's top gets first sun-touch in the continental U.S. every day. U.S., here's where you meet the sun each day. If clouds don't balk it. (It's said Quoddy Head, eastern most point of U.S. land, vies for this honor.)

Back on the highway. Crossing into Benedictia, the Aroostook County line.

Stop in Houlton highway welcome center, check email, let Allen know I am safe. Downtown Houlton seems to be dropping out of the plan. Should I let it get away this time?

The tent is up—Aroostook River Campground outside Presque Isle; I should be relieved—am when the wind blows. So hot and faint-like. Heavyheaded.

Uplands Interlude

The AMC view. The river's down there somewhere in the pucker-brush and trees.

Thank you for the chair in the small shade, the breeze. Please give me another cloud.

The flies buzz, good old blue bottles—they don't bite. What to do now? Gazing out at the view across the hot dusty green river valley, August Green. Can't think. Will try to read, brave the sun to get a book. *Literary Journalism*, I think. A car slows by. Better wait for a cloud. Where's my sunglasses? But I did not think I'd get the tent up, either. The poles kept popping out, coming apart.

Sign on the church I'd passed on Route 1: Where are you headed? I don't know.—Where? Are there any surprises for You?

Can't possibly write. Wish I could work on *Isildur's Bane*.

Fetched up the book to read. Thank you for helping me. Thanks for the cloud. You have so much. How do you keep track of it, keep it all going? What makes you want to? Is it ecstasy—that thing you share with us sometimes—rarely and but the merest taste?

Cumulo-cloudy-breezy. Think I'm heat-drifting. The car is wide open, its wings and flaps and gate thrown out. It should take off, but it just sits.

I had wanted an open campsite, not thinking too much of the sun and its affect on me. Oh me. The too-skimpy shade.

But it is very beautiful big, far horizon, trimmed all in white and green. The hills are as I remember, Ohioan. Wooded and meadowed and full of grain or potatoes. There are trails here but—keep wondering if I'll get to them. So want to . . . but—20° cooler and I'm there. Good breeze now, warm. Not too too warm now. And the shade keeps getting bigger as the sun downs, earth slopes away. No one is moving. Campsites with travel trailers, but the place seems deserted. I like it.

Should try to get ice. Don't feel like moving.

The leaf shadows flicker and jump. Sunlight, spotting the page, moves about. This tree is dancing with the breeze while rooted.

"The American Man at Age Ten"—10-year-old Colin when asked, What's the most important thing in the world? 'Game Boy.' Pause for a personal response. *The world. The most important thing in the world is the world.*—Or, is it a boy?

Turned on the AC, sat in the car; drove into town, got summer wheat beer—went to the Presque Isle library, checked e-mail—Allen asked if I found the wheat—should have said *yes*—but wasn't thinking. His "wheat" is a reference not to beer but to the metaphoric wheat we searched for at the airport—World War II era transport—all those years ago. See the earlier Aroostook, Uplands travel account. He desired the living pulse of that place and time. It's now but a cloud of witness.

Sitting on the picnic table—not as clean as it might be. Bird doo. This is the time of the gold-green Aroostook light. Pleasant, and would be peaceful if the buzz saw would stop. They are working on the campground. Wish I could turn to the horizon but the sun is there, still hot if setting.

I look over my finds. For one dollar at the Presque Isle library I got *Dorothy Day: A Radical Devotion* by Robert Coles. The cover picture, her countenance . . . looks . . . old, broken, sad, intellectual. I know almost nothing about her. But that should change now. Coles, on Day, says she could not sleep for reading Dostoyevsky. That Tennyson moved her to passionate "romantic anguish." Passages of Scripture stood out—as meant for her. (Page 21.)

Day thinks deeply, and seems always to have done so, about the "ordinary" things of life. A sampling: Her consternation and wonder at how God keeps track of All, so much ongoing with billions of people a'borning and dying, more being born again. God keeps track Of All. And I've heard Allen wondering the same thing. I think, God must also, through faith, keep track of every subatomic particle and its concomitant invisible "somethingness"—I do not say nothingness. And orchestrate everything all at once, perhaps out of what a moment ago had no appearance whatever. Coles' corresponding thought of the gigantic computer makes me think of *Bruce Almighty*. But Allen has said it is more than that . . . in its *personal* dimension. God is relating to us or with us momently, as one Person to one person. I go a bit further or deeper into the miracle to say that Jesus, the God-man, is doing this. With each of us individually all the time, as Maledil with the innocent green lady in *Perelandra*. "There is a friend that sticketh closer than a brother." People cannot understand how he might do this simultaneously with everybody . . . and so these people never think about it at all. I think: people inured to being in touch with everybody in the world through the Internet, unable to believe in God's own, and compassing, personal interest and contact? Our ancestors could not have believed in something as fantastic as the internet, as social media, but they could believe in God's personal and social attention. In Coles' book, Dorothy Day is shown believing that people pray through how they live their lives, their

Uplands Interlude

work ongoing, their friendships, love offered and received from people. Is the only form of prayer *words*?

Just *being* with a troubled soul is a prayer for him or her. We may like to see our words or presence bring someone out of trouble, set them in a happier frame, see the effort fruitful. But that is not our business. The power of verbal prayer, says Day, is no more powerful than merest presence. Making a mess of things and struggling over it can be a form of prayer. Struggling to care is prayer. Not caring is also a form of prayer. A negative prayer: God, don't make me care.

More Day: Interesting thoughts on idealism as expression-gathering in a soul over time. . . . But also as received inspiration. A gift. With responsibility to treasure it.

We also face temptations, of which we may be unaware, to sour the gift. Embrace cynicism, dampen the ideal in others. We forget to watch, and slide into the mental morass, mental custom. Dr. Johnson went to Devon to escape his "custom"—his customary ways, slothful and otherwise bad, in order to strengthen his "habits." The sea contrasted these terms for him: *customs* with *habits*. In the book on her life I will pick up, cheap, further along in the month at our local library, Simone Weil is shown learning that so-called habit is not, as we normally think, something enchaining, but something freeing. Custom enslaves, but habit is the self-possession springing from its exercise.

For free I got audiotapes of *Pillar of Fire* by Taylor Branch, to keep company with the journey on the road home. This kind of reading/listening makes good companionship, good thought life . . . but does it really acculturate *me*, my own being? Does it help me *be* better? Can one act better without being so? Is this what CS Lewis is getting at when he encourages us to pretend? Of course pretending can be seen as hypocritical if the pretence is not sacrificial. One sits thoughtfully still, holding someone's hand with hope . . . when one would rather be running away to the surf.

Facing a pillar head of fire, the lowering sun, with my hat brim turned, shielding and low. I should see stars tonight. The rolling hillside, and far lonesome barking of dog. The saw has stopped.

What am I doing here?

How people lived was enormously interesting to Dorothy Day, wrote Coles. She thought deeply, often,—how ought one to live and how respond to others struggling with the question. (p. xxi.)

Visiting the Eastern Uplands

Orange sun crowns the Aroostook hill/ridge opposite, going, going.

Went on the dusky golden bike ride—these green mown grass trails—to the back of beyond. Penetrating to the mystery past all the campsites, up into the interior realms, dimming green. So very buggy here on the edge of beyond. Oh! these tall grasses and fireweed and purple loose strife. It is another, secluded, green and delightfully deliberate mazelike world I see in here, daring not to stop among these clouds of blood-eaters. Lower down, deep toward the river the sun is gone—but a corner—and then the dark violent glowing of its furnace. Oh the mosquitoes have a feast! I've helped with the propagation—another rich cycle. . . fed on my blood.

Now the clouds above are dusky dark. Were I at the back of beyond I would no longer see the clouds of mosquitoes—nor the trail. Now, the sky above the ridge across the valley is an early night/ late evening blue. Yes I like it.

. . . Here, in Aroostook, after the day's exertions, struggles, puzzlement, dismay. The edges of western clouds and bottoms are all fuchsia and fusing with deep violet/charcoal. I hear the near and far sounds of folk settling, tiny remote voices. I seem the only one with a tent. All have their little traveling houses, caravans they call them in England. The folks three sites away have a smoky campfire. They need it—no doubt. They are backed into the woods. Soon the mosquitoes will find me from the long long grasses edging my site.

Then it's the tent for me. Yeah.

But what about the stars? Will the mosquitoes put the sting into them? I'm writing along, I guess, but not on *IB*. I can hardly see the words.

Suddenly it's quiet.

Slow-Boating Aroostook in Air

In the a.m., Rob's Pit Stop after biking rts.167/163. Got here just before the rain shower. Watch it plinking in the lot. And after coffee in my moose cup supplied by neighboring campers, he a carpenter over from Portage, for which mention see the first section of the Aroostook journal (from nearly two decades ago). He said building is all over Maine since 9/11. People looking to get away from the city, any city, he may be thinking.

Fresh dewy foggy early morning, the sun eventually beaming over the campground from Quoggy Jo Hill behind. The Pit Stop is brand-new with

Uplands Interlude

racing/Budweiser motif. A store of convenience for everyone and self. Hope the infrared-warm sandwich will feel itself comfortable all chewed up in my stomach. A bottle of juice. New England Coffee Roasters coffee—kind of an oxymoron (to me). So good this morning.

Would like to hear the neighbor tell how Portage has changed—will ask if opportunity arises, but I sense the cold shoulder coming. Indeed I think it has already knocked me askew. Last night I was invited for morning coffee but that changed to retraction after I had opened my ungainly mouth. Her poor spouse having to deliver the message, with the coffee this a.m.!

Forgot to mention the short white clover all over the ground of the campsites. It is so open, free, uncluttered and plain wonderful. But the heat dismays me. Must finish here at Rob's, and bike while cool is cool.

Am sorry I did not get to experience midnight and moon, the stars last night. Hope I will toughen up tonight and do it. I pray! I was cold!!? And felt the trip to pee would make me colder. Cold concrete floor in there. Seems I'm not so good at roughing it. . . .

Rolling and wooded. Fields, hills, the green.

Notes made on the road: biking down the highway a giant bug-like machine—watering? Fertilizing by spraying, trying for disease-resistance? Its arms a grid-work, a lattice erector-set folded forward.

After 5 p.m.

Clouded over, bit stagnant, but thanks *much*!

Guess books and their reading aren't all I've cracked them up to be. Back to the dollar shelves at the library and found *A Movable Feast*, Countess Tolstoy's diary and literary notes. The former, by Hemingway, is very good reading. Not profound, but putting me there in Paris in the 1920s with him. Gladys Hasty Carroll's *To Remember Forever*, copyright 1963, an account of her sophomore year at Bates College, 1925; and *Barchester Towers* with *the Warden* together in one book—have never read any of these. Dipped into the first two beneath our shade tree . . . so enriched in these finds, thank you. . . .

Reading in the hot evening under a small tree in this high Aroostook River Campground. I tend to recollect places where books are commenced, or my reading of any part, if the setting is not usual to me. Then these wonderful settings are conjured again—in the way that place or time is—as

Visiting the Eastern Uplands

with a particular musical composition experienced away from the place and time of its initial hearing.

And, dipping into the *Diary of Tolstoy's Wife*, who says of love: "Never, indeed, through all my life, has *aimer* meant an emotional game to me, but always something akin to suffering." And she quotes Tolstoy: "Fatalism is an excuse for doing evil." Also says that the wedding scene in *Anna Karenina* is her own.

Then, after a couple hours reading, felt so lonesome and empty. Allen.

Felt I had to move. Act. Be active even shortly, briefly. Went down, through the short grass paths, to see if they have 'puter for guests to check e-mail. Nope. The library was suggested. . . . Hmm. Must have heard of me telling the neighbors they seemed workaholics. What's rude or negative about that?

Feeling raindrops as I sit now at the picnic table with cheese, beer (small wheat—yum) and big black grapes. Hope it stays off till I finish . . . but I can do with a few such drops. Thanks.

Hot bike ride the a.m., uphill, searching for a different way back, and met kind folks, had conversations about family reunions and making things. In fact, I was invited to the coming family reunion. I returned the same way, though something in me does not like returning over the same ground. The adventure must pursue. Be circular. A circle back is as good, in venturing, as going a straight line away from somewhere, whether campground or home.

Allen how I wish you were here. So lonesome. Strange. What am I doing here? Got your e-mail at the library—so glad—but I don't recall your message! I'm ready to vacate in the a.m., but still can't help hoping for a surprise from God. That is, guess I'll go home if I don't get one! Or, if I do.

Crepuscular rays, shades of which look dirty in shafting to the Ohio-wooded ridge. Its sides in green and potatoes, in distance beyond the out-of-sight Aroostook River.

Went down to the River today before coming back to the campsite. Found a trail paralleling the river. For snow machines, but it seems to be an old settlers' road, old River Road. The four-wheelers must use it also. Goes all the way to Caribou and back the other way toward Presque Isle.

I saw the strange-insect-looking machine in action on a potato field today and made a note. Looks like a great bug, and I wonder if they copied one to make it on its long legs with wheels that leave almost no trace in the flowering potato field. Or have the potato flowers gone by? Machines

Uplands Interlude

and systems copied from nature are best. Think of the vascular system as a template for routing traffic on limited access highways. Or Velcro copied from bees knees.

Borrowed a scrub brush, bucket, and detergent to wash the picnic table. At first I was going to buy a tablecloth at the owner's suggestion but I thought—what? Cover up bird poop?

If it rains tonight and I have to pee? I'm going out white-naked and doing it in the yard (sez I now).

Have I read the Carroll book, a journal, maybe, before? The *To Remember Forever* by Carroll is a definite Maine book, written from lengthy notes made by her sophomore self when she was a Hasty. A memoir of leaving home in the 1920s to go to Bates College, and—so far—how this was accomplished. Told with warmth, deep caring of all she had known to that time. A firm sense of the language. Her innocence and good will come through with the natural restraint of her time and folks. South Berwick, also home of Sarah Orne Jewett. And germane to the Aroostook experience, because Carroll's was a farm household and ancestral background which she used in her *As the Earth Turns*. A most excellent Maine novel. I cannot imagine Carroll or anyone then being assigned reading that would offend sensibility, taste, or morality—or even morale—not while at the Academy in South Berwick. Even at Bates, they went to chapel each day.

Two motorized hang-gliders—ultralights—are just passing directly over my picnic table, not very high. Both flyers wave when they notice me watching here below. It's a sign! I'm to take up hang-gliding—in the Aroostook air! They crossed the river in the trees below and are going out of sight. . . . Now almost out of sound . . . in the direction of Caribou, north.

I'm reading, drinking beer. A half-hour, 20 minutes—? 45?—They are back. They look funny in profile, slow-boating it over the hills. Quoggy Jo. Now they seem just below some of the treetops toward the river. One is dawdling somewhere beyond, humming-slowing, seems to be turning back. And I recall the Maxi Anderson Memorial and the *Double Eagle* and Presque Isle where launched the first successful transatlantic balloon; of excesses and economies of travel.

Mosquitoes just starting. The sky completely clouded, gray-blue. Everything in nature, but that bit of man, humming and slowing and humming again. Lawn-boy easy-riders in the sky.

Getting a bit lonesome again. Reading Gladys Hasty Carroll, *To Remember Forever*. Girl Power.

Visiting the Eastern Uplands

Girl Power

"Girl Power" is the big hammer-shaped balloon the young girl at Myrtle Trees Farm was dubbin' round with yesterday. Almost as big as herself. Almost. She was just a bit like I was, that age—possessed of the half sullen, half bored mood of a child some might like to smack sense into . . . until one recalls the same would apply to oneself.

"It's full of air," I said. "Is there any power in air?" For some reason this query brought her back to normalcy. It gave her pause, thought, and a brief half-quizzical smile.

(Oneself?—I thought of the "prince-of-the-power-of-the-air," Socrates, and some other things in the space of that half-friendly moment.)

Then, at leaving, I started thinking about it, really. Air is breath. Oxygen is respiration of trees; CO_2 is of mammals, etc. Breath, more like spirit, is powerful enough to keep us alive, to keep the world alive. Wonder what *she* ended up thinking about?

Ended yesterday with a long walk up the road into the stagnant and somewhat dirty dusk of the "Ohio" backroad. It paralleled the Aroostook River which I could not see for trees below the road. Farmhouses, houses, sheds, barns. Rising across the river a quarry, sand and gravel and maybe rock. Trying to satisfy my restiveness and ultimately succeed, especially after a quick shower. The neighbor who had retracted a coffee date—though she did send coffee over to me via hapless (kind) husband along with her retraction—was in the bathhouse rather closely watching over her grandkids. Pointedly, she did not glare at me. (Read, *not glance*.)

There was also a German couple at the campground—don't know if they have left, since the late-night early-morning rain. Young, with small children who called often to their parents though they kept right together. Could hear father and son in the showers next the women's bathhouse. These showers share a wall and the ceiling is open. A little girl: and mother of the two small girls—the one was constant in her cries for Mother who was right there or maybe but a few steps away. I felt the little girl's strangeness—she felt the strangeness of the place and desired constant vocal assurance. And on the one hand it's irritating. On the other it reminds me of, well, me and God. Are you still there God? . . . still there? . . . now are you?

Quite irritating. But I keep thinking—that is us, our condition. We are children. Life, being, is *strange*. Mom and Dad are comforting.

Uplands Interlude

Busy morning after rain preparing to leave. But drive into Presque Isle waiting for the tent to dry out; get some coffee, breakfast, then bring order to the messy car in the lot at McDonald's.

There, while inside the fast food restaurant, I spy a couple perusing my Maine Atlas. They've moved it from its place over to their table while I was in the restroom.

"That'll cost you 25 cents!" (No Mainer me.)

They look up laughing, and the conversation begins. New Yorkers. Of course. That's why they are friendly. Open and easy in rural Maine. Because they are not Mainers. (Bad bad writer, tsk.)

A sprightly conversation about travels and camping in Maine. I am asked if I'm traveling, camping alone.

After a moment's hesitation, "Sometimes."

The woman's smile deepens. A knowing look supplanting the other, but not unfriendly, smile.

She has it wrong, but I'm not clarifying it for her. They have got almost all my secrets from me—that I took off on the spur of the moment after my spouse left the state on a job. . . . But the "sometimes" is my secret.

"Sometimes" means *sometimes* I feel God with me, *sometimes* not. It also means, I don't know you well enough yet to trust you, so it's best you not think me traveling alone.

Saw some Amish! Driving horse and buggy!—About to cross in front of the drive-through window.—And I nearly forgot to stop for the coffee after paying. The horse and buggy, dark plain homespun, long skirts, broad brimmed hats, beards.

The girl at the window found them "awesome" and said they had a community in Oakfield. I had heard of this, had wanted to check it out, and decided to . . . perhaps. . . . If I can find the right back roads.

Nothing accords like the Amish with the themes of *The County*, especially as I have used Ohio. . . . As, in part, originating from Ohio. There they are running out of affordable land for their sprawling extended families. Some have gone to South America, some to Aroostook County, where they had not been seen before. Not even at the time of our first trip's account in these pages. . . . I will but drive through, see the seedling roads south of here, not so well kept as where there is motorized farm machinery. . . . Where mostly the rumor of Amish condenses up like dew through grass

Visiting the Eastern Uplands

and soil. They are a secret here, not too badly kept. And I will not be writing of them now, I think.

Checked the e-mail, got situated with Allen, regarding plans to meet. Went back to the Aroostook River Campground and struck camp—have I always wanted to write that?—well maybe not. But it felt good writing it, so maybe? I had been comfortable in that tiny tent, sprawled out alone. The new camping mattress was a complete hit.

Myrtle Tree Farm was like another world. The work of great artistry that does not mentioned its own artistry. Or, in other words, it's not *artificial*. I was going to take pictures and buy something. I had hinted I'd come back for it. But I did not. Girl Power is still there for all I know. A charity case, I think she was. Anyone would look bored or sullen. Charity can do that to a person. Or charity can brighten all—every one of—our days. Come, Charity. . . . Are you there? . . . Charity? Not sullen, me.

Seven hours. Long long long drive home. Companioning the *Pillar of Fire.* Amazing contrast of power-grabbing Elijah Muhammad with the age's great martyr, MLK. I feel strongly the pathos of Malcolm X.'s disjunction. What if he had been a disciple of "The King?" But Malcolm X. proved to be the conscience of what were then called the Black Muslims, and the story of these lives and times would not have been so good without him.

Route 2 is torture for the impatient. But very beautiful. These Maine roads need fixing—*BADLY*. Potholes, patching, dips and ruts on a main Maine state route. Nourished my soul a bit at the tail end going through Peru, the wilderness of Dicksville Rd. past Concord Pond through Milton.

Overall impression of changes in Presque Isle? Since 1990 (thereabouts): it's been stripped-malled, busier, more traffic. Perhaps the statistics have changed; road notes of the demographer, in which Aroostook County was then the only one to lose population.

Home, Waiting

What about this? Commands are not rules. Commands are laws—like the law of gravity. . . . Our nature is another unbreakable law in conflict with these unbreakable moral laws. . . . Are we ourselves inviolable, the expression of fallen nature in conflict with that of the commandment? I have

Uplands Interlude

written in conflict, but could that just as well be "in concert?" Conflict in the concert?—in the personal operatic version of creation? What would Tolkien say? But he has Eru already saying it in *The Music of the Aniur*.

"What is me? I'm no thinker." But I know my experience. I know what I am in this experience... and long to know what I will be in *the other*—the resurrected life. This is not mine to manage or know—another law? Or is the longing itself part of the law of the fallen nature?

I'm home, waiting. The travel journal entries are a mess. Built a pile of rough notes. Too introspective, not enough Aroostook. No proper travelogue.

Reading the *Before the Trumpet*, FDR's early years, over breakfast, bought off the library used-book rack in Presque Isle. Trying, today, to bring order. To be very hot, sticky. A smug day.

Took *Isildur's Bane* to Aroostook with me intending to write but did not crack it once. In fact, I was surprised to see it among the books I brought up from the car along with the tent, blankets, dirty clothes, etc..

I recognize some of the things Hemingway says about the process of writing, especially harebrained things, capriciousness. He was writing of these 30 plus years after the fact of his experiences. The poet John Chico Martin says that the present has no historiography. It is our writing these things down, here and now in this moment, which bequeaths it to what is past—here meaning my Aroostook travels. Writing makes it historical. That is why it's so important to fix the memory right, in as much detail and veracity as possible, note-taking. Without the pen precision is elusive. So is verbatim.

Washed the tent, hung sleeping bags and rain-fly out to air. Emptied the car. Composting. Found peppers, two kinds, in the compost pile! Brought into the house and washed. Put them into the crisper. Emptied the dishwasher. Kitchen a mess all day and since Sunday.

Waiting for mom to call, 6 p.m., eating char-broiled burger and garden salad with garden basil. Sent Nance an e-mail. Worked on *IB*!!—824 words... from 12:30 to 3:30, maybe 4 p.m., including transcription. Voice-recognition transcription, something I did not have writing the first part of *Visiting the Eastern Uplands*. Allen is not yet home.

Ohio, Maine. Again

August 1, 2015

IN THE FIRST PART of this book, as we traveled south toward Houlton near the end of our trip, Allen and I talked about perspective and perception. He said that returning over the same ground reinforces what we've seen along the way. Yet, in this new episode we have an inversion returning northward, one set in a further time and for this reason yielding a different point of view. Our perception is altered, our understanding more complex and mature.

Today we are two and half decades north in the metaphor. We are older. Are we wiser? At this moment we have about two hundred miles under our belt today. We are again in the Eastern Uplands at a place called Mountain Glory Farm just outside Patten—a farming and logging community in Penobscot County since the beginning. Its beginning.

We sit parked outside the farmhouse in rain, blowing, bucketing, surrounded. Thunder, lightning. The impressionistic image of an Amish household down the lane beyond the windshield, rain shield. An old apple orchard, in the back yard of the guest farmhouse we are to stay in; in the back quarter we see the tree boles misshapen, dark leaves upturned and pressing heavenward. We are here for two days, three nights, in Ohio, Maine.

The land here is like Ohio—deeply rolling, like an ocean, green, standing still. Rural Ohio and the Eastern Uplands of Maine. *Boom!!* There is a difference, however. That would be *Katahdin* in the distance, beyond the woods. The Greatest Mountain, risen in the state of Maine. Nothing like it in Ohio. Ohio is where we got caught Maine Fever—in a reversal of the historic and fabled movement of this state's populace from Maine to Ohio (in the late 1800s CE).

OHIO, MAINE. AGAIN

Christina Shipps, who owns "Farm" apartments and the business of renting them to visitors like us, was from New York City before coming to Maine. She bought and renovated two properties, iconic of Maine traditions: the seaside Victorian harbor resort house, and this uplands farm. This 1890s farmhouse is now a duplex for visitors interested in quiet, in spaciousness and peace. She discovered these 170 acres in winter, stopping on the edges of farm and woodland, between great Katahdin—white, isolated, silent—and Lumber-land. Snow laden trees and fields: Woodlands rolled out from where she stood, whitened, rising and falling, with the greatest mountain magnificent above and beyond.

August 2, 2015 Sunday a.m.

Depressed and discouraged on account of wet feet. Fridge is off after a power outage. The power came back on but the fridge stayed off. So our food needs cooking, how do we eat at all? This would not be a problem for our Amish neighbors.

Now I understand the saying. It comes from the *literal* wet feet, no metaphor: We walked the Farm and meadow loops—the former last night, the latter a bit ago. My shoes and socks are soaked, the only shoes I brought. My injured, now aged feet and their decidedly necessary orthotics are wet through. Disruption, depression ensues.

Such a beautiful but dewy a.m., drenching our feet. Wild appley, poppley, thick sprucely blue and green. What I feel like—blue and green. Thank God for sunlight—bright! After the drenching! Greenly and blue, drying everything.

We are staying on Mountain Glory Farm. The Amish are here, very quietly. This is an Ohio view from the back weathered deck of an old farmhouse converted to apartments, north and south by name. There across the pasturage are rear ends of black-and-white milkers glimpsed through trees beyond the meadow. Maybe they are eating apples. Is there now a wild apple forest over there? Thick. Thick. The tails do flicker in and out among green leaves.

Allen went into the house to get the Amish pocketbook guide. There are maybe three books on the Amish here. Our hostess, however, is not Amish nor has she ever been. The Amish come not from New York City. (Hah!) Besides the guide, there are maybe three books about the Amish on a coffee table by the couch.

Visiting the Eastern Uplands

I first saw the anomaly of an Amish man in Maine while standing on the mezzanine in L.L. Bean's. I stood . . . gazing at the Amish man. I had been in L.L. Bean's many times and never seen one there. The Amish, as I thought then, were in the Midwest, Ohio (where we used to visit "Amish country"); they were in Pennsylvania; some in Canada. I thought there was a range of Anabaptists, from the Mennonite to the Old Order Amish. This man was definitely of the Old Order, hat and beard. And standing in L.L. Bean's on the mezzanine, quietly observing everything. Everything. As he was in turn observed by me. *He, however, was not surprised by his observations of L.L. Bean's.*

Apparently in reversal of the state's history, some Amish have caught Maine Fever. Christina Shipps had completed her guest house project when the Old Order Amish began to move into this part of Maine from Ohio. She invited a young Amish married couple to build a new dwelling with barn on her property, completing the hoped-for working farm. Here they bring up a young family. The Amish community worked together in a "frolic" to raise the barn, much as our farming ancestors did with their communal "barn-raising." Forty or fifty Amish men worked together on the building, and the women, as you might suppose, fed them.

As guests we've been asked (in a flyer) to "observe a few courtesies." Looking them over, I see that these are courtesies it would be good to extend to anyone, and to receive oneself. But the first request is also part of their religious belief—that they do not appear in photographic images. So Christina Shipps asks that guests not photograph the Amish nor ask permission to photograph. The farm and animals and views are all freely offered for image gathering. Animals are not to be fed, and this is another rule that any animal owner would like to see observed with regard to their domestic pets and farm animals. Our host reminds us that the Amish work very hard without electricity, machinery, motorized vehicles or other equipment, and they are raising children, so time is precious. She asks that we not engage them in long conversation and even suggests that a friendly wave can be a perfect way to acknowledge one another. We are to respect their private homes and properties. Fortunately, Christina has apparently hired a mower to make paths for walking about the broader reaches of the farm.

Biked in Patten yesterday after burgers at the clam shack (I know). Surprising, the traffic of small rural communities. More so where we live in the mountains. We came home to walk the Farm loop path and saw the great ghost of Katahdin upon reaching Christina's lawn, a great meadow beside her elegant new house. Here she first saw the greatest Mountain on her visit to the woods. Snowmobiling. I long to snowshoe here.

Socks and shoes are on the railing in sunlight. Ravens call. Beyond the meadow, tails swish in the apple wood.

It was a reset button on the wall socket behind the fridge. Yesterday power was out from a lightning strike nearby—but the village was out as well. We discovered this on our bike ride, heard private portable generators outside each house.

Allen at the weathered table behind me is reading one of the Amish books. This one written by a professor formerly Amish. As he opened the book I glimpsed a musical staff in its pages.

After breakfast (made in "our" kitchen) we biked Wildflower Lane—the Farm-loop-reverse of yesterday. We noted the neatly cut hay-rows, an upended wooden flatbed trailer. Empty on the Sabbath in the middle of the lane.

Then biking round back roads outside Patten village with its friendly-looking neighborhoods, houses together, comfortable and neat, one of which (we'll notice tomorrow) is being refurbished by Amish carpenters. Mass is being celebrated today, we noted, at the small Catholic church. Everyone entering dressed in their best. Back to the Clam Shop, across from the community recreation center, ball fields, playground—for yummy burgers (again). Craig's Clam Shop. Coleslaw too sweet, but oh those burgers. Post Meridian. Drive to Island Falls. Some kind of community 'do ongoing. We wanted to bike but it was too hot, so plan a return tomorrow.

Allen spies a monarch butterfly from the deck—he says the fifth-generation it is, time for the return to Mexico this autumn. He likes milkweed for these butterflies, would plant some in our ditch above the drain field back home.

The breeze picks up, clouding across the vast Ohio-Maine sky.

Allen goes off with his Sony digital camera to picture the great brown draft horse. We saw it early a.m. on our dewy walk—between two close-grown tall, shading but thin-stemmed apple trees. Picturesque.

On our return from our Island Falls outing a very small Amish boy—wearing what looked like a dark suit with dark hat—gladly waved, and called "Hi!" hoping for our own glad return. Twice! It was fun and joyful. Especially on his part, and I can but linger over it, hopeful in my aging.

Clouding more. Now still. Very quiet here, now a dirt bike (I think) goes past, leaving silence in its listening wake.

He got it!! The picture Allen wanted this morning! He went and stood just beyond the trees, and the draft horse, curious, came over and took his place as hoped! Cannot lose these exclamation marks, oh no. (!) He did not want the clouds, but they insisted.

Now the sun is back, the clouds drift apart and whiten. Fat, dark-bottoms, still, drifting peaceably. The power will stay on?

Now the breeze is back, as well. A leafy shadow shaking, the real leaves a'rustle.

Allen wants to ask the Amish how they moved their buggies from Ohio. But we will not ask. As a suggested courtesy, we respect our hostess's request for limited conversation. For one thing, we are at leisure. They are constantly at work. (Except today.) This day is a day of rest, a Sabbath for both the Amish and us. Less and less and now, seemingly, there is almost no Sabbath for "the English."—The *Englischer,* in Amish terms, are all cultures except their own. They speak English, but in the first five years of life they speak dialect of German. The little boy who cried to us and waved, initially cried, "Hi!" to practice his English. And I cried back "hello!" He imitated the cry. He is under five, maybe three years old.

My own question for the Amish would be medical. Are there Amish doctors? What, if anything, do they do for illness? For illness unto death? Three questions I wonder over greatly, imagining answers like those our ancestors would give.

Personally, I *fear* the medical industrial complex, that is, I fear captivity to it, and want to be completely free. Not free of illness, nor free of death, yet I wonder what that decision does to my family, should death be not swift. What turmoil would that throw them into? This is why the living will I have made, now with intent to frame upon the study wall. Is the extended family to be the ante-room to the final resting place for the Amish? And, do they bury their dead on their farmland, perhaps even nourishing future generations? And I would say with them, *For me it will not be the extended round of medical procedure*, diagnostic equipment, the agony of trying to keep this form alive. For me the victorious peace of death.

How did Christina Shipps come to speak to the Amish woman with whom she made arrangements about the Farm? Christina is the one who informs her guests, if not in person, then in the literature: it's courteous to speak

Ohio, Maine. Again

little with them, and on inconsequential topics (what we mostly use with other strangers—how about this weather?) She writes, "Their dedication to family life guides their decisions about where to live and what occupation to pursue. . . and much, if not most, of an Amish person's life revolves around their large extended families." They obey the (literal) biblical teachings and decisions of the Amish Congregational elders. It is given them to rebuke those who stray from their commitments.

Inside the house I find a copy of *House Calls and Hitching Posts*. Walking out to the deck, I look it over. Reminiscent of my Ohio youth, the screen door slams behind. *Stories from* Dr. *Elton Lehman's Career among the Amish*, as told to Dorcas Sharp Hoover (living with her spouse in Dover, Ohio). This doctor delivered four of the author's children in his birthing center. But, despite her name, Dorcas is not Amish. The publisher is Good Books, Intercourse, Pennsylvania. I may find some answers in this book. Doctor Lehman practices in Wayne County, Ohio, the county we lived in before leaving Ohio. His answers are not from Maine, but from Ohio. I may ask Christina about this deeply concerning question—if I get the chance. A quick skim here shows the good doctor working on the mutilated hand of a young Amish man, who arrived with his hand in a kerosene can and appeared to need no anesthetic. Such accidents can happen in the harvest season.

Turkey vultures? Apparently circling, sailing on late afternoon thermals. The great white clouds a heaven heaping above flat gray bottoms, the green orchard branches above green mown grass beneath the dappling shadows. *Glorious God!*

The bumbley bees have been so busy about the nameless flowering ground cover, hundreds, hundreds. They are small colorful many-handed acrobats over these pale gray blossoms, fluffy cumulus of leafy flowering.

Clip-clomping, returning our friendly waves, the Old Order Amish family just drove past on the lane toward farmhouse and barn. (We are still out on the deck.) I *think* these may be Sabbath day visitors. Women driving the small wagon, younger men in back, facing rearward, smiling, waving in response. Allen talks with me about the difference between Old Order and Mennonites. He's looking at *A Pocket Guide to Amish Life* by Mindy Stearns Clark, Harvest House Publishers. We talk briefly about coming back in winter, wintertime snowshoeing. Perfect for that. The meadow and farm loops. Imagine the pristine solitude, quiet, the crisp tracking through snowfall, leaving great webbed prints behind. I keep hoping, but, apparently, we can't leave our snug log house in the winter western mountains long enough. We heat with wood.

Monday, August 3, 2015 Mountain Glory Farm, 4:15 a.m.

"In the beginning was the *Word*. And the Word was with God, and the Word was God."

"And God said, there must be *Light!*"

"The same was in the beginning with God."

We plan to go to Smyrna after Island Falls, and then on to Houlton. We visited Houlton on our first trip, 25 years ago. These places are in Aroostook County. "The County," bordering Penobscot County with its village of Patten, in the rural town named for Amos Patten.

Biking in the Town of Crystal early, biking the extreme Ohio hills. The paradox is that in our own Maine western mountains we don't usually find the hill-riding this extreme. Our roads and lanes curve around hills and mountains through valleys, alongside rivers, streams. Now we push our bikes up, slide down between high fields and woodlands. And some newer houses. *Up up up up. Down down down down.* Repeat. Mostly we don't pedal . . . but push bikes up then glide back down. The wind in the bright a.m.!

But there is *Katahdin* over there, as I write later in the p.m. on the deck in great dry warm wind. Voluminous! Papers from our day's travels blowing away! The great mountain rises ghostlike or solid depending on the weather, its weather—amid these rolling Ohio hills. Greatest Mountain in Maine, terminus of the Appalachian Trail. In Thoreau's day few whites had climbed the mountain before him. (Evidently Amos Patten was one of these in 1804.) Today its trails may be continually scattered with people ascending, descending. Thoreau's prediction was that this would be so, and long in the coming. The spelling of its name, meaning "highest land" in the Abenaki tongue, varies. He wrote it *Ktaadn*. It was a disturbing place and experience for him. "We had our first, but a partial view of Ktaadn, its summit veiled in clouds, like a dark isthmus in that quarter, connecting the heavens with the earth." His language is particularly expressive of his experience with the mountain, as he said elsewhere, "The night shut down at last, not a little deepened by the dark side of Ktaadn, which, like a permanent shadow, reared itself from the eastern bank."

I've quoted him on the mountain elsewhere, a powerful evocation of the stern stone giant. (It might be well to mention the Abol Trail here. Because the treacherous Abol Slide was finally closed this summer and there are no plans to reopen it soon. For many decades this slow continuous landslide, thought even to have been used by Thoreau in his ascent of the mountain, has been called a trail; though in truth, it is an unending river of descending talus or stones. I have written elsewhere of my experience with it 30 years ago. The trail I tried to climb, the evil slide, has since been closed as a dangerous ascent. . . .

At Smyrna Mills we stopped to ask directions at the low, long structure housing an Amish shed-building concern. We were seeking an Amish-run store in Smyrna. We pulled in, chatted with an Amishman happening past in the parking lot. Conversation, as a courtesy is to be unobtrusive, but at some point, I asked about something pertaining to the Amish alone—with an apology. Something—which, in this mighty wind out here on the deck writing up my notes—I cannot now recall. I cannot give a play-by-play of our conversation; only highlights, conversational points I remember. He was middle-aged but youthful, courteous, brown-bearded, friendly, and totally unoffended, expressing the last in no uncertain words. He wore a straw hat on account of the heat. Would it be off his head in this fierce south wind we have now on this deck where I push my pen?

He turned out, to my surprise, to be something of a proselytizer—with a little booklet. This needs careful nuancing, in both writing and reading. He was not, of course, talking about us joining the Amish community. He confirmed my impression that Amish included a range of adherents to the community way—from Mennonite to Old Order. He was of the latter. Nor was he going to talk to us about becoming Christians. We had brief exchange on, *What is a Christian?* I suggested one who talks to God like a human being, as though God is a Person—as in Christ. Yet, on reading the booklet much later (at home), I found something necessarily more. But, at

Monday, August 3, 2015 Mountain Glory Farm, 4:15 a.m.

that conversational point in the parking lot, if the term *Christian* was not defined as one hearing, and speaking with, Christ? What then?

Because, he did ask if we were Christians.

When he had his answer, he kept talking in this direction. It became evident that without the affirmative answer, he would have stopped talking there. Possibly bid us a friendly farewell. Instead, because of my answer, he began talking briefly, person to persons, about our times. I recall particular words, "consume" and "persecution." I said Allen and I must be consumers, gesturing toward the sleek lines of our three-year-old Odyssey.

Now, sitting on the farmhouse deck in this wind, I'm recalling something from the first part of this book on our upland adventures, written in the autumn of 1990. Back then I had scarcely begun to hear the word "consumer." True! I used it in writing about our early Aroostook encounters. Scarcely, had I begun to realize what it meant. I thought, back then, of using it in place of, or as a form of, "materialist." You see here how terms change in 25 years. This word *consumer* is vastly more expressive of what is today in this part of the world, maybe in all suburban and metropolitan parts, *The Way* of life.

(*Clop clop clop*. Haywagon goes past on the lane. *Loaded*. How did they do that? Three thin Amishmen, two of which are young, and this wagonload, the second since our return, looking like a mountain, engulfing these thin harvesters. It is a mountainous harvest. And now I recall the hay rows, lying trimly after rain as we walked down Wildflower Lane, and oh how this dry wind must be drying all that harvest. How did they pile it up in this furnace-blasting wind? Remember, the Amish. They have no baler. They pitch it loose and dry onto the flatbed—pile it, and pile it, pile. How did they keep it altogether? Keep it from blowing past in the pitching? Did they have to lie down on it after each pitch-forkful to keep it all from blowing away?)

So, when asked, we say, yes. Yes, we would like a copy of the little booklet written for Christians. He may not have said—I have the impression that he is the booklet's author. He walks off to get one from the shed-construction building. Reading later I will find that the Christian is *not* solely one who talks to God, and that this kind of fellowship is incomplete—not completely Christian—according to scripture (and this agreeing little booklet).

On his return with the booklet, Allen asks another question, with apologetic preface. This one I remember. Allen asks if he is from Ohio. But no. He is from the further Midwest, Missouri and Minnesota. He did not even see Ohio until his mid-twenties.

Sitting on the deck overlooking orchard and pasture, I see, on the back of the printed booklet handwritten in blue ink, "Jonas Yoder." I don't yet know what's in this little booklet, *Christ's Message to the American Christians*. I do not think it will sound alien to me, or entirely unfamiliar. And I remember specifically his reiteration of the scripture that before "the end" there will come "a falling away." He said something like: There are Christians in great variety the world over. By this I think he meant multiethnic, multicultural believers in Christ. I remember this Amishmen saying that *even . . . some* Amish are not Christians, not believers in Christ. This mystery may be solved for me on reading the booklet.

So that was our surprise conversation with an Amishman.

What I would like now is to see our neighboring Amishmen unload the wagon in their community-raised barn. But I won't. I won't walk over to watch, calling attention to myself and what they're doing. Though . . . were I invisible I'd relish seeing it. However, if they take it out empty to the harvest again? I may climb on my bike to follow distantly after, find the field with rows of drying harvest on Wildflower Lane. See just how that hay is loaded in this blasting wind. It must be harder than sitting here on this deck, papers anchored with cups of coffee, pen whittling its way across the travel-journal page, attempting visions.

Dimly, I recall a prophetic read once—something about the grain, the wheat, being already loaded, the harvest was in. This was back in the early 1970s, written if I remember right in the late 60's by an AWOL (absent without leave) on hunger strike in prison. However, a prophecy is not a literal or legal prophecy until it is shown fulfilled. (Is it too late to *believe* then?)

You want to explain the difference between writing this stuff and *being* this stuff. Yes, I'm talking to myself here with the pen. I should try a metaphor of the hydrologist who studies the history of water but is not consciously water though largely (physically) made up of water.

I write *about* what I believe. I write *what* I believe. But do I live, act on, it? And is it true belief if I do not? Belief has not yet destroyed my fallen-ness. My sin nature lives, though it's said (quoting the apostle Paul) I am crucified. Jesus has not yet re-created me in his likeness. In my fallen-ness I am morally didactic—as it is *felt* today. And perhaps in spirit, I am. Often

Monday, August 3, 2015 Mountain Glory Farm, 4:15 a.m.

I sense a self-righteous spirit in me, pride with all its roots entwined and wrapping round the sinews of my soul. Didacticism, early, meant "to teach," to point out with digits of the human finger. I can make a story but cannot *teach* how to make a story. I cannot make my own being a good story for God. Oppositely, paradoxically, I can point a digitized moral in storytelling, but, though I cannot teach morality as Jesus did, it is all I write. It's just here in this pen on the deck as I write. Even as I am its target.

I quote from Henry David Thoreau in these Maine Metaphor books. He was a writerly self-crafting blowhard (as I am). But self was not his main subject. We don't and can't know the whole story about him. So far in my reading of him, foremost he is a writer. Except for what his contemporaries have to say (who were also crafting him), that's about it for us. He was a wordsmith who crafted his character flaws. For which I admire him. Repentance is not much noticeable in these flawed-character acknowledgments. Or is it?

Was he nature's naturalist? I don't think so. He loved nature and handcrafted her secondhand with his pen because he was a creative writer, desiring not so much the factual as the *mythological*. His journaling, he wrote, "should be material to the mythology I am writing." He was crafting a voice. His experiences were material to work with. June 18, 1840: "I'm startled when I consider how little I am *actually* concerned about the things I write in my journal." The self is worthy of satire because another name for it is pride. (I disagree with those who use Self as a synonym for Soul. Soul is the person within the body, the psyche—emotion, intellect, personality, will. Self is the devil. Note the distinction of capitalization: It is not destruction of the Self but destruction of the Soul we want to escape. Selfishness is the devil, ego, pride disguised as something meaningful.)

While he seems humorless sometimes, even seriously hardened, I suspect Thoreau of self-satirizing. I'm not a scholar or critic and my reading maybe suspect: It may be that God is satirizing him. I would not put it past God to do this. Because I'm fairly certain God satirizes me.

On the Military Road to Houlton?

As we rode down-highway on our way back to the western mountains and home, I was still wondering about Military Street, also Military Road, and making notations about our side trip to Houlton next to the Canadian border. I needed to contemplate roads and civil divisions.

Following our interview with the Amishman, Allen had gone into the Amish-run establishment in Smyrna to look around. The store was lit with skylights, but candelabra lighting was available through kerosene piping for dark days. Aisles were dim, with mote-shot rays from overhead, aisles full of tools and other items for use off the electric grid—hand tools and appliances. At home we are equipped, fairly, for life off the grid with a hand-pump and portable clothes washer with hand-wringer, kerosene, etc. But we live on the grid except during outages. By the door of the Amish-run establishment was a bookshelf for Amish cookery. I have regretted not going in with him, since.

After visiting the Amish-run store on the highway passing through rural Smyrna, we headed east toward Houlton on Route 2. Was this roadway laid overtop Maine's old Military Road, layer upon layer? Also, I had wanted to compare today's Houlton with what we saw 25 years ago. In the event, we found it much the same. But it's what you want. I do. . . . (More on this to follow.)

I wrote briefly in our *Experience in the Western Mountains* about Maine's minor civil divisions, and how they are open to change by a vote of residents. In the Mountains of Western Maine, the Town of Albany, for instance, decided to stop being the Town of Albany and became the less structured Albany Township. I will explain the difference below. Town boards in these instances are disbanded, services paid by town tax revenue are locally dissolved, and parents of children may choose where to drive their kids for

On the Military Road to Houlton?

their schooling, paid for by the State, taxpayers of the state, into which local residents are also paying. Maine also has plantations, example Dennistown Plantation; and Surpluses, example Andover West Surplus. Some townships are numbered, that is, having a number for name: T14, R5, sometimes with a few uppercase letters appended (T14, R5 WELS). The name signifies the number of the Township and range, with further place designation. WELS is short for "West of the Easterly Line of the State." Population in these townships are found in the *Maine Atlas and Gazetteer* open on my lap as we drive along; making me wonder because they don't seem to agree with letter-size: *Atlas* towns that should be of a size, but are not:

Most Towns have villages and hamlets, either or both, and these will be centers of commerce, services, schools, and local government for those within the rural town boundary—the geographically much larger surrounding woodland and agricultural countryside. I'm using the *Atlas* as we drive along toward Smyrna, and it is meant to have font sizes clueing one to the size of these town-related villages with regard to population count. The larger the font size, the greater the population, supposedly. And I have in the past found this letter-size useful. So, looking at the names of Patten and Smyrna Mills, I was expecting a village size comparable with that of Patten. Because of corresponding letter-size written on the map, against our expectation, we blinked and Smyrna Mills never showed. It was meant to be the size of Patten with Patten's gracious neighborhoods. Maybe, like Brigadoon, Smyrna Mills is hiding among folds of the Maine Uplands for the next hundred years? Or perhaps the town center was off somewhere in the woods? Route 2's Island Falls is also showing like size with regard to font. Using *Atlas* font size can be deceiving because, as we head toward Houlton, I see Houlton showing neighborhood streets and intersections of state and federal highways, and yet the font looks of a size with Smyrna Mills. How can this be, we're thinking, as we blink and Smyrna Mills is gone.

Houlton has a creatively laid out town center, much as it was in 1886 when a history was written for *A Gazetteer of the State of Maine*. It feels like an Aroostook small town, an Ohio small town, as described earlier in this my still percolating Eastern Uplands book. It reminds me of Ravenna, Ohio where my son was born, or any Midwestern small town. Here Main Street and Military Street converge at the triangular town "square."

After parking on Main Street behind the courthouse, we step into the County Co-Op and Farm Store. Looking for coffee, finding an attractive abundance of food grown and preserved with care, things made by hand, and—at the moment—a friendly and quiet atmosphere. People are ordering and eating freshly made pastries. Allen orders a blueberry scone. When it arrives, he generously gives me what I ask for, a taste. It is rich and dense and not too sweet, this scone. I'm trying to refrain from ordering one for myself.

This is an old-time interior, with stamped tin ceiling, a gallery above on three sides, its railing supported by spindles of lathe-turned wood, showing the grain of trees grown 100+ years ago, and felled by the ax. I receive friendly permission to take photographs. The Gazetteer, in 1886, tells of starch factories, cheese factories, a canning factory, woolen mill, four lumber and three flour mills, a couple of iron foundries and other industry. Particularly, I like that it mentions the "overall well shaded and very attractive streets," That's what I saw 25 years ago—and what we see here today surrounding town-center.

My glance falls on the *Houlton Pioneer Times* headline: "Cary Plantation moves forward with plan to dissolve town." I pick it up. Below the story is another smaller font headline with separate article: "Bancroft completes three-year process to disband." The town of Bancroft was founded in 1889 and ceased as of July 8 of this year, 2015. The process involved shifting its governance and management from Bancroft and its residents to its new guardians, the major civil divisions of County (Aroostook), and the State of Maine. I pick up the paper, head toward the cash register.

Christopher Burns writes an excellent article in this *Houlton Pioneer Times*, in-depth and explicating all the twists and turns of this process. He writes that, during the past 100 years, 41 towns in Maine have closed their town halls (wherein all town stewardship occurs), and were disorganized as local entities. Sixty residents, in this latest instance, ceded their responsibilities for governance nine years after the 26-person populace of Centreville, Washington County, forfeited theirs. Rising property taxes necessary to support infrastructure is the reason for disbanding. Local roads, bridges, schools and stewardship maintenance costs have escalated beyond what they can afford. Maine's population is aging, and with fixed incomes. The aging of the community overall shows me that youth is abandoning these parts in search of work and life, as has often been the case in other parts of Maine (and until 2001 with its 911 scare, this was so everywhere rurally). Thus, funds needed for schools and other services are going away.

On the Military Road to Houlton?

I wrote in the first part of this uplands book that Aroostook was the only County to lose population as the State, in the late 1980s, early 1990s, finally grew past one million residents! (According to the U.S. Census). Professor of geography, Eldred Rolfe, taught his Maine geography students that state population had grown at a quicker *rate*, from 1784 to 1820, than ever before or since. Apparently the trend continues. The long process for Bancroft involved thinking about where to vote in the future; about its liquidation of assets; and about State handling in rules of the unorganized territories. All were considered.

Are Maine's eastern upland rural Towns in need of new residents? That would depend, in my own thoughts and concerns, on what *kind* of new residents. I think mainly of income, its sources, and especially of the moral qualities new residents might bring. I'm thinking of Christina Shipps. If the wealthy were to come here, they may bring controlling thoughtless tyranny. If newcomers are nonworking poor, an additional burden. Other considerations are less important, or maybe of no importance. Ethnicity, for instance, is of no importance. The Amish, however, seem a complementary and well-integrated population here, on account of moral qualities, including work ethic. These qualities are highly reminiscent of qualities found in Maine's founding, and in the founding of these rural towns. But, given my own thoughts and concerns, still, I have no say. I can only watch, and witness. And I will.

My attention was directed to a couple old black-and-white photos of this shop on the walls. Here we see the same patterned tin ceiling and balcony but with poised people in the background on the ground floor, very still yet somehow candid. The clerk at the counter wears contemporaneous puffy sleeves with embroidered bodice. Their posture and look are not like the stilted poses of the late 1800s we usually see. One image, I notice on viewing after our return home, is suggestively spooky, whether from my digital mishandling or . . . other . . . extra bodily . . . communicatory properties? . . . Perhaps confirmed by the rather dreamy look in the pictured clerk's eyes? Whatever the reason, it came off my camera virtually with ghostly finish, particularly in one spot by her elbow: There a quintet of wee people glow mistily with surrounding aura—or is it a standup advertisement?—

In the *Story of Houlton*, by Cora Carpenter Putnam and published through House of Falmouth in 1958—that's where I'll learn about the United States Military Road and how it was worked into existence. I'd studied this before in my Maine history class under Professor Richard Condon and was glad to refresh my memory with this story and quotation from historical documents, one from a February 1831 report of the state legislature on state lands. Of course the road was built by the military, a corduroy road made out of logs, destined to be repaired again and again. I still need to confirm if this was part of Route 2, Route 2a, or something other entirely. I would like to know if I have traveled over part of that road, on any of my Aroostook journeys. We're told the reason for this primitive road was to provide for a northern outpost, when there were Canadian-US northern boundary disputes during a 30-year period. The Military Road was a boon to the area, opening it to settlement and woods-rural industry beyond what the Joseph and Sarah Putnam Houltons had begun as a family. But, when the Mexican War began, the military was withdrawn from this area.

When I got back home I e-mailed Linda Faucher, the Gary Library librarian at Houlton, who kindly scanned some pages of the 1958 book by the wife of a descendent of Houlton founder, Joseph Houlton who (along with Aaron Putnam), pioneered in 1807 before statehood. She also sent me definitive information, from the Maine Encyclopedia online, about routes 2 and 2a being overlaid atop the Military Road. "A military road (roughly following the current U.S. Route 2 to Macwahoc, then U.S. Route 2A to Houlton) was authorized to aid in the movement of troops from Bangor to Houlton." So, it turns out we went over the eastern heroic and historic route years before in our travels through Aroostook County, but, on this journey, we did not drive the road which helped bring this part of Maine into a Massachusetts district settlement. Route 2a lay to the east of our road this trip. In additional web browsing I find, via Wikipedia, that Houlton is the birthplace of Samantha Smith, the child who brought peace to the Cold War through the written word. This town is the county seat of Aroostook County, especially liked by me for its nickname—the "Shire Town."

Moving Southwest beneath the Sun

WRITING ON TUESDAY, AUGUST 4, 2015—Driving home, on Maine I-95, back to the western mountains, my pen driving across the page. . . .

. . . After early biking Wildflower Lane: In the a.m., seeing where the hay was harvested. And we captured images of Katahdin from the owner's front lawn—where Christina Shipps receives the view commanded by Katahdin. But we had missed our best photographic opportunity, for the best view was two days previous in the morning. Rock-sides, adamant, pale, were then visible as bold stone—instead of the contoured mountain silhouette, the ghostly shaping of itself. In rephrasing that old saying about the river—The Greatest Mountain appears never twice the same.

We then drove to Patten to bike one last time. Biking, collecting neighborhoods, community center park, the newest find: Love Joy Road, just beyond, an extension of Station Street. Going out and up into fields, potato and alfalfa, the stray house. Landscape opening, road becoming dirt, then puddled. "*Uh-oh*," escapes me. A dark dog runs out, tearing the turf. *Grrrr. Ruff-ruff-woof!*

Breakfast at Debbie's Deli, corned beef hash, eggs over medium, sausages, home fries. Coffee. Coffee. Friendliness.

Even here west of Bangor, pen working, heading toward Maine Route 2, it's Ohio! Fields and crops and sky and clouds, all blooming, drying for the harvest. From I-95, catching hold of the state route 2.

So wishing I might have seen the young Amishmen loading their haywagon in that fierce, implacable, persistent wind. Hay mountain in each load, carrying also the harvesters, bouncing, clattering, and two puppies bounding after.

August 5, 2015, home in the western mountains.

What I like about writing is the distinct passage into concentration. Especially as I age. I disappear in writing, or transcribing; or when I read. Reading the work of others is a passage into concentration, as well as into another land. Into friendships. I like reading and writing very very much.

What I do not like about writing is what might be called extra-craft. Outside the crafting. Today that would be marketing, and what people want to think about the crafter. All *Maine Metaphor* books were crafted, at the beginning, in middle-age, and three are still in progress as I near the end of living in these mountains, in this world. The real sinner is writing, crafting, escaping in the act. Sometimes I am daunted in writing lest others mistake the crafting for the person.

I love the Eastern Uplands. There is much food here. But I am afraid.

Here are loose ends neatly tied: Christina Shipps provided answers for our questions. We wanted to know how the Amish family came to live and frolic and work the farm. I find her method rather bold. She chased down an Amishman in a buggy and, when he stopped, asked if there were more members of this new Amish community yet in Ohio who did not have money for a farm but wanted to come to Maine. Thus began a dialogue with this Amish family to use Shipps' farmland. It was his daughter and her husband who came, with buggies and everything else taken apart and shipped here in a truck. In demonstration of Amish uses of modern industrial equipment, they rode the bus to Maine. The Amish decide, not as individuals, what they will adapt to their way, and how—whether long term or temporary.

The Amishman's little booklet, delivered into our hands while we talked, was not written by the Amishman. I contacted the author on finishing my reading of the booklet at home, one Roger Hertzler of Watchman Gospel Signs in Oregon. He confirmed that the booklet had been ordered by Jonas Yoder.

Apparently the booklet confirms what Jesus says of himself and his followers in the Gospels. Here's where it gets interesting. I did a Scriptural word search in order to find out what a Christian is. The search shows a Christian is one who *obeys* the Lord Jesus Christ. In the Book of Matthew he says that heaven and earth will pass away but not his words. A search on "my words" will reveal much about this specific definition.

A new light has been cast on prophetic words for me. I'm thinking of the *little* book mentioned in John's Revelation, last of the canon. You saw my reference in the occasional modifier *little* coupled with Jonas Yoder's gift of the little booklet. But now, as I write these words, I'm thinking of something more.

What if I couple the Gospels themselves (along with Jesus' words), to liken them to the experience of John upon receiving the little book in *Revelation of Jesus Christ*? You see, the good news to me is very sweet and has been all my life. For me the Gospels are the revelation of the Lord Jesus Christ. I'm to be saved by believing what Jesus says. But now, correlated with this suddenly outstanding command to obey, and my deterioration and aging. . . . And with such changes as have happened since we began our Aroostook quest 25 years ago . . . namely the increasing corruption of this world as seen in our disastrous fornicating consumer, surveillance, and terrorist culture. . . . The books of the good news are becoming increasingly bitter. I've had Time to experience everything given me in life to experience, especially Self . . . and am perhaps leery of yet more Time. That's where the bitterness is—*digesting* the real message of the good news.

The good news is love. And love has been from the foundation of the world. Then and There Christ crucified himself in the making of all . . . and He, the astonishing word, sacrificed himself in the flesh later (as we might say). And we are in crucifixion with him. Self-sacrifice is the good news. Read about the qualities of love in Corinthians and you will see. That is very bitter to Self, is it not?

Until all is made new again in reality. Reality. Not in a metaphor or symbol.

I don't know what today will bring. Do you?
Hope, I hope. For one thing.
Some lightness, some levity, good will.
Some of the colors, reds, yellows, orange, on leaves and trees
and the passing way of flowers in autumn.
But hope.
Some days that's all we want. . . beside our needs.
These beautiful things, lively. Alive with the presence
of greatness creating it all. A friend. Be my friend?
I'll be yours.

www.ingramcontent.com/pod-product-compliance
Lightning Source LLC
Chambersburg PA
CBHW060821190426
43197CB00038B/2173